The Tropical Marine Aquarium

The Tropical Marine Aquarium

Vincent B. Hargreaves

A DAVID & CHARLES BOOK

For Lee

Page 2: Jewelled Grouper (*Cephalopholis miniatus*) photographed at a depth of 35ft off the Kenya coast. This fish is 1ft long; juvenile specimens are suitable for an aquarium but larger ones are best left on the reef.

British Library Cataloguing in Publication Data

Hargreaves, Vincent B.
  The tropical marine aquarium — 2nd ed.
  1. Tropical marine aquariums. Fish.
  Amateurs' manuals
  I. Title
  639.3′42

ISBN 0-7153-9375-8

Typeset by H B M Typesetting Limited   Chorley   Lancs
Colour reproduction by Gilchrist Brothers Limited   Leeds
and printed in Hong Kong
for David & Charles Publishers plc
Brunel House   Newton Abbot   Devon

Distributed in the United States of America
by Sterling Publishing Co, Inc.
2 Park Ave, New York, NY10016

Contents

List of Illustrations

PART 2

PART 3

Introduction

The keeping of coral fishes as a hobby dates back to the turn of the century. However, only in the last twenty years has it become a really practical proposition. These days the cost of maintaining a marine aquarium is little more than it is for a freshwater aquarium.

This book will, I hope, start the newcomer to this fascinating hobby on the road to success, but will also provide the experienced aquarist with a useful source of identification and reference.

Coral fishes and invertebrates provide an incomparable spectacle of colour, life and movement in the comfort of your own home. It should always be remembered, though, that if these creatures are to be kept successfully it is essential to learn as much as possible about them. The hobby continues to grow, with more and more technical knowledge being applied each year. This applies particularly in the case of new filtration methods and of coral fish-breeding procedures.

When I first began to research and write this book, and much more recently to revise it for this new edition, I became aware of the enormous technological advances that have been made in marine fish keeping. It must be remembered, however, that the basic rules of good aquarium management remain the same.

I hope that this book will introduce many people to this wonderful and rewarding hobby.

Vincent B. Hargreaves

(*All photographs not otherwise acknowledged are from the author's collection*)

Part 1
Setting up the
Aquarium

Clown Triggerfish (*Balistoides conspiculum*)

Setting up the Aquarium

The setting up and installing of a marine tank requires some forethought and planning. It is advisable to start with the largest tank possible as anything under 20 gallons (90 litres) capacity is of little use to the beginner. This is because the volume of seawater in a tank is directly proportionate to the number of fish that can be housed and the rate at which the water will become polluted. This is unfortunate in some cases, but it is a fact that seawater is far more unstable than freshwater

The tank

The introduction, in recent years, of silicone sealers and subsequently all-glass tanks is perhaps the most important breakthrough for the marine hobby. They make fine marine aquaria and have been proven to be extremely sturdy and non-toxic to marine fishes. There are many shapes into which one can make an all-glass tank : triangular, square, or even hexagonal. They are also available ready-made.

If the reader decides that he would like to have a go at making one, he will require : glass of suitable sizes and thicknesses, a roll of adhesive tape and a tube of silicone sealer. The pieces of glass should be taped together to form an open-topped box, and the silicone sealer applied to all the inside seams. It should then be allowed to cure for forty-eight hours, after which the tape can be removed. If the sealer manufacturers' instructions have been carried out to the letter, the result should be a perfectly water-tight container, provided the glass is strong enough to withstand the weight of the water.

As an alternative an ordinary angle-iron tank can be used. The drawback with this method is that salt water corrodes the frame and the tank soon becomes unsightly. However, this problem can be overcome if the tank is sealed with silicone on the inside seams. The top part of the frame that normally comes into contact with the water can be given two or three coats of epoxy resin, or a good quality polyurethane paint.

It should be noted here that whilst an angle-iron is not necessarily toxic to marine fishes, steel, zinc, aluminium and aquarium putty are. So great care should be taken to ensure that any water that has come into contact with these materials is not allowed to drop back into the tank.

Plastic aquaria are satisfactory, except that they have the disadvantage of being easily scratched and are seldom available in sizes large enough to accommodate more than one or two fish. Nylon- or plastic-coated frames are acceptable, when glazed properly, but care should be taken when handling the plastic type as they chip very easily. Nylon frames are superior but a little more expensive.

Whatever type of tank is used, it should be rinsed out with a strong solution of potassium permanganate or methylene blue to sterilise it. It should then be placed on a firm base—away from direct sunlight or heat from radiators or fires, otherwise the water will overheat.

Aeration

A wide range of pumps are available these days, some of which are suitable and others less so. What is required is a quiet, robust pump giving the maximum possible output. The normal pump has a vibrator action and this type is extremely robust and cheap to run. Alternatively the piston pump, although noisier, usually produces a larger output.

Whichever pump is chosen, they all perform the same function—producing air either to power filters or to be dissipated in the water via an airstone.

If an air-pump is quiet when new, yet becomes progressively noisier over a few months, then this usually means that the diaphragm needs changing. These items of equipment are inexpensive and are normally easy to replace. There is no doubt that it is better to do this than put up with excessive noise week after week until the pump fails completely. Apart from changing the diaphragm, the pump will need occasional servicing to keep it trouble-free and it is a good idea to follow the manufacturers' instructions on this point.

Salt water absorbs considerably less oxygen from the atmosphere than does fresh water. On top of this, the normal marine fish's oxygen requirement is some 200 or more times greater than its freshwater counterpart. Water absorbs oxygen from the air, but only to a depth of $\frac{1}{8}$in (3mm) so that the surface layer quickly becomes saturated with oxygen and must be cycled in order to let a fresh layer of unsaturated water reach the surface. That is the job of the air-pump, and the faster it creates this movement the more oxygenated the water becomes. That is why all marine tanks have large amounts of air being pumped 'through' the water. I use the term 'through' the water to stress the fact that oxygen is not magically pumped *into* the water by an air-pump, the air-pump only assists the natural process of oxygen absorption.

A canister filter

Filtration

This is possibly the most controversial aspect of marine fish keeping. Briefly, there are three ways of filtering a tank and thereby supporting life in it. These methods have been popularly named (or mis-named) : the natural method, the clinical method, and the semi-natural method. Of these three life support systems the last is more successful and reliable than the other two. Most of this chapter is therefore devoted to explaining how the semi-natural method works. Before this, though, a general outline of the other two systems is given.

The natural method
The natural method involves using no artificial filtration at all. Live coral and rocks containing marine worms and micro animals, bivalves, such as seashells, and plants and algae, are all contained in the aquarium and are used as a natural filter. Airstones are used to keep the water circulating and so preventing stagnation. It is a tricky way of keeping fish but it has the advantage of easier maintenance of difficult fish and low cost.

The clinical method
Tanks filtered by this method can prove quite healthy for fish if they are set up and maintained correctly. The clinical system involves using high-powered electro-mechanical filters which take the water out of the aquarium, pass it through activated charcoal and filter wool and then return it again.

The problem with this method is that because only the water is filtered a good thick base medium cannot be used, otherwise food and excreta would become lodged there and could decompose to produce poisonous gases. Therefore any potentially toxic substance must be removed immediately.

Apart from frequent water changes, ozone reactors and ultra-violet sterilisers are often used, along with protein skimmers (these are dealt with later), all utilised to produce gin-clear and unfortunately plankton-free water. Needless to say, it can be an expensive set-up, using money that could possibly be better spent on fishes.

The semi-natural method –
The biological filter

The low cost and easy maintenance of this system make it a very attractive proposition. More solid plus-factors are the low failure rate of aquarists using it and the numerous breeding achievements recorded. So it would appear that as far as marine fish keeping is concerned, undergravel filters will be around for a long time.

The basic set-up is simple: a high-powered undergravel filter, covering the floor of the tank completely, is used. This has the effect, when it is operational, of purifying every square inch of gravel, and consequently leaving no 'black spots' where uneaten food and excreta can decay and produce nitrogenous toxins.

The term 'high power' refers to the rate—in gallons or litres per hour—at which water is passed through the filter medium. (It is not correct to refer to water being filtered *clean* at 'X' number of gallons per hour, as this would depend on 1: the maturity of the filter medium, and therefore its potential as a means of removing poisonous matter; and 2: the state of the water itself. It is correct to say, though, that the *turnover rate* of the undergravel filter is 'X' number of gallons per hour.)

The filter itself can be bought off the shelf or made to your own specifications. It consists of a porous corrugated base-plate (Fig. 1) the size of the inside base of the tank, with one or more outflow tubes of a height determined by the depth of water in the aquarium.

In the base of the outflow is inserted the air-line running from an air-pump (Fig. 2). When the pump is running and the tank is filled with water an 'air-lift' action takes place, pushing the water out of the top of the tube as the bubbles strive to reach the surface. Water is drawn into the tube from the space between the filter base and the bottom glass. This causes the water to flow down through the gravel and the porous base-plate, replacing the water

Although fairly hardy, even species such as this *Abudefduf oxyodon* will succumb to inadequate filtration

which is being drawn off, and so the cycle begins.

The 'turnover rate' is normally determined by three factors: the amount of air pumped into the filter tube, the number of tubes, and the internal diameter of the tube itself. An increase in any one of these parameters will have the effect of increasing the turnover rate of the filter.

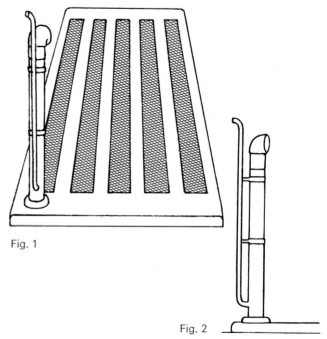

Fig. 1

Fig. 2

What the filter does

Pollution is caused by uneaten food, excreta and other alien matter breaking down into nitrogen gas and then forming nitrites. Even small pieces of food left in the tank will cause a build-up of nitrites because nitrites are accumulative. This, as one can appreciate, happens in freshwater tanks also. But most freshwater fish can stand greater nitrite levels—up to 200 to 300 parts per million—whereas some marine fish start showing distress at only 10ppm.

Many marine aquarium disasters can be attributed to this and the lack of adequate means to test for it. What nitrites do is to cause the fish to become weak and prone to disease, and if left exposed to them they lower the fishes' ability to remove oxygen from the water until they eventually suffocate.

Pollution can be avoided on a long-term basis by the use of an undergravel filter.

How biological filtration is achieved

To ensure that the undergravel filtration system is capable of breaking down organic wastes into inert solids, such as *nitrates* (not to be confused with nitrites)—so that these can be utilised as food for plants such as algae—the filter must be allowed to 'mature'.

Maturation is achieved by the natural process of allowing bacteria colonies to begin forming in the gravel. This can be assisted by providing a good depth of base medium on the filter bed. The composition of this is described on page 16.

Preparations containing freeze-dried bacterial cultures, which assist specific bacterial growth, are now being produced commercially and these go a long way towards making the marine aquarists' job a lot easier. Normally, though, bacterial growth in the filter medium, caused by uneaten food and excrement, will occur as a direct result of feeding fishes in the tank.

There are two types of bacterial colonies which may form in the gravel and these are labelled 'aerobic' and 'anaerobic' (ie pathogenic). Aerobic bacteria thrive on oxygen and break down organic wastes into inert solids, but pathogenic bacteria do not and usually cause disease. Aerobic bacteria colonies in the gravel, therefore, are very desirable, but pathogenic are not.

In order to ensure that aerobic bacteria are formed in the gravel they must be encouraged to do so. This is done by providing adequate aeration, since oxygen acts as a poison to anerobic bacteria.

Omnilogical filtration

So long as the marine aquarium is exposed to enough light to allow green algae to form during the maturation period then omnilogical filtration will occur naturally.

Green algae is important in a marine aquarium; apart from utilising nitrates, it also encourages aerobic bacteria by producing oxygen—as indeed all plants do.

Algae, which were once thought to be undesirable in a marine tank, have now been proved to be of extreme value to the aquarist, completing the chain in the life-support system.

Maturation of a marine aquarium

The time taken for a biological filtration system to mature is usually between seven and sixty days. During this time an excessive nitrite build-up normally occurs particularly when fish are included in the tank. For this reason it is advisable to include only hardier species of fishes, such as Damselfishes, and even these—during the nitrite phase—may succumb to disease. Once this phase is over the tank will settle down and from then on only extreme carelessness will upset the balance of the system.

The nitrite test kit

This kit measures the amount of nitrogen in the water in milligrams per litre. This provides a fairly accurate guide to the nitrite level using the conversion ratio: 1mg of nitrogen = 3·3mg of nitrite.

The kit usually consists of a sample vial, reagent additives and clear instructions on how to test a sample of the aquarium water. A means of comparing the colour of the water under test against a calibrated chart is also included.

Base medium

If the aquarist is using anything other than undergravel filtration the only courses open to him are: to use very little base medium, none at all, or one of the new artificially made 'coral reefs'. These come in prefabricated units and can be used to create quite a pleasing effect in an otherwise barren tank. They are usually manufactured out of fibreglass, moulded and coloured, with pieces of dead coral mounted into the base to create a natural appearance.

There are many types of material that one can use to cover the floor of a tank and the following list is made up of those that have been tried and proven in marine aquaria:

Crushed shell
Aquarium gravel (not artificially coloured)
Crushed coral
Silica sand
Coral sand (Oolite)

If the aquarist has decided to use a high-power undergravel filter then it is suggested that he combine two or more of these materials to form layers. A 2in (50mm) layer of fairly course crushed shell can be spread over the base of the filter, followed by 1in (25mm) of aquarium gravel ($\frac{1}{8}$in or 3mm grade), or crushed coral, then finally covered with $\frac{1}{2}$in (13mm) of coral or silica sand. This, once matured, will be a most effective filter medium, although there are several combinations which are just as good. The aquarist should bear in mind, though, that fine silica sand or coral sand will be sucked through the filter and ejected through the outlet tube if it is not separated from the base by a good layer of course medium.

For the undergravel filter to give good results a depth of *at least* 3in (75mm) of base medium should be used.

Apart from the undergravel filter there are several other systems which employ the same air-lift principle. These take on a variety of shapes and sizes but all use the same type of filter medium: nylon wool and activated charcoal. The latter has the effect of absorbing certain toxic gases present in the aquaria, and may be used in layers along with nylon wool in the filter box. With all these filters it is a good idea to encourage algae to grow in the filter box and so provide additional omnilogical filtration.

The nitrate test kit

In addition to the nitrite test kit previously described, a new test kit has recently been introduced onto the market: the nitrate test kit.

Although nitrates are inert solids and, in controlled amounts, harmless to marine life, there comes a time in a closed system, such as a marine tank, when the build-up of nitrates exceeds the 'nitrate tolerance' of the inhabitants. The time taken for a system to reach lethal saturation depends on several factors, not the least of which is the fishes' own ability to withstand a particular level of nitrate build-up. For instance, delicate species such as *Zanclus canescens* or *Chaetodon trifasciatus* cannot withstand a higher concentration than 20ppm nitrate, whilst hardy species such as the Demoiselles can withstand up to 50ppm. Thankfully, the aquarist now has the means to test this level.

There are several ways of lowering the nitrate reading; the most obvious being to simply reduce the stocking level of the tank. Or, if the aquarist does not want to do this, he can slightly reduce the amount of food he feeds his fish. This alone will not lower the nitrate reading, unless there is a certain amount of plant-life present in the tank. This is because plants absorb nitrate from the water. Regular algae 'harvesting' will also prevent the level from building up too fast. Lastly, the nitrate level can be reduced by changing part of the water.

Ancillary equipment

Lighting

Incandescent, quartz halogen or fluorescent illumination can be used, although the latter is preferable because it produces a uniform light without bright or dull spots in the tank. Whilst a striplight is initially more expensive, the actual running cost is cheaper than with an ordinary light bulb.

Fluorescent light units designed to produce light with a colour rendering towards the red end of the colour spectrum, whilst being ideal for promoting good algal growth and enhancing the colours of certain species of fishes, *may* be harmful to marine fishes and invertebrates on a long-term basis. A theory that this type of light is ultimately damaging to the eyesight of certain species of fishes has yet to be proved or disproved. However, there is nothing to stop their use alongside normal fluorescent lights on a 'two normal to one special' basis, but a lighting system resembling true daylight is preferable and is normally less expensive. A simplified spectrum analysis is shown below to illustrate the point.

The conventional method of illuminating a tank is by the use of a hood that fits neatly on top. Hoods are often made of aluminium, and as this oxidises on contact with salt water and becomes toxic to fishes, it should be given a good coat of polyurethane paint or a cover should be fitted—a sheet of glass or clear plastic which is cut to fit the top of the tank. The cover serves the dual purpose of keeping the splashes of water away from the metal hood and light fittings and also acting as a condensation shield to cut down the loss of water through evaporation.

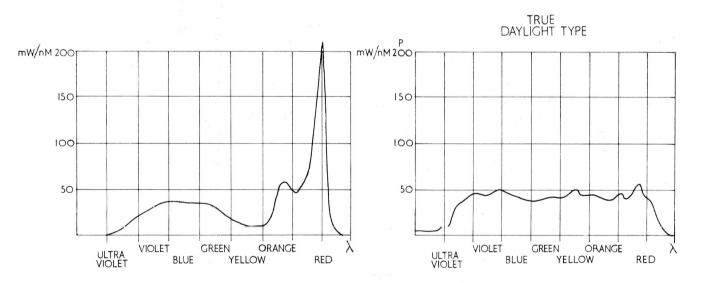

This spectrum analysis demonstrates the difference between natural light and fluorescent light

Quartz halogen illumination

For the aquarist wishing to encourage algal growth, propagate the higher algaes such as *Caulerpa sp.* or to keep invertebrate animals with any degree of success, quartz halogen lighting can be of considerable help. Anemones in particular seem to fare much better in a tank using this system. The main feature is its high penetration which in terms of an aquarium means that more light reaches a greater depth.

This type of lighting is also useful in large aquariums or those of abnormal depth.

Above: The good growth of algae is beneficial for assisting filtration

Right: Coral fishes in their natural habitat: a coral reef off the Seychelles
Photo: Heather Angel

Controlled heating

It is important to maintain a stable water temperature in a marine aquarium. At one time this was very difficult, but the advent of glass and recently silicone-cased immersion heaters and thermostats has virtually eliminated this problem.

These days all commercially available heaters, thermostats or combination equipment (both units in one tube) must conform with certain safety regulations. Thankfully this has produced a range of equipment of a very high standard so that the purchaser need not worry about the reliability of one type or another.

Coral fishes should be kept in water at a temperature somewhere between 23° and 26°C (73°–79°F), but an effort should be made to keep it around the 25°C (76°F) mark, as this is the ideal level for most species. Most heaters nowadays have plastic or silicone stoppers but there are some still around using rubber ones which rot quite quickly in salt water (a little silicone sealer can be used to cover the rubber). This locks the cap and seals it, preventing seepage of water into the tube. It also applies to thermostats, unless they are of the outside fitting type.

These external thermostats usually have a metal clip that fits on the inside of the tank, but it is no problem to render it safe by threading the clip through a length of plastic tubing before fitting it onto the frame.

Heaters and thermostats combined in one tube are available, and these have the advantage of being more reliable and allow easy access to the temperature regulator.

When choosing the size of the heater one should allow one watt per litre (or 100w for a 20 gallon or 90-litre tank).

Thermometers

Most thermometers are sold with rubber suckers, which should immediately be replaced by plastic ones. Thermometers that stick on the outside of the glass are now available and are much neater than the internal type, and just as accurate, though a little more expensive.

A tip to remember when purchasing a thermometer is to hold several in your hand for a few seconds and then check the temperatures. If there is one that differs from the rest it should be avoided as it is probably faulty.

The protein skimmer

This inexpensive piece of equipment is used, particularly in the clinical aquarium, in order to confine as much as possible the organic waste. It operates on an air-lift principle and is placed inside the tank. Water is drawn up the central tube and is allowed, by the design of the skimmer, to bubble over, leaving a proteinous deposit in a small compartment above the water surface. This compartment is usually removable for cleaning. It is quite effective but by no means foolproof as it is only designed to reduce, not eliminate, proteinous matter in an aquarium. Therefore, depending on the number of fishes, etc, a gradual build-up of organic pollution can occur.

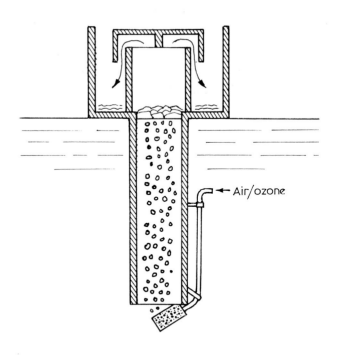

The protein skimmer

The ozone reactor

When oxygen is passed through an electric field it forms an unstable gas called ozone. This poisonous gas, in controlled doses, can be extremely beneficial to marine fishes because of its ability to kill bacteria. The ozone reactor supplies these controlled doses and can be used as a supplement to an undergravel filter, but care must be taken to ensure that the outlet tube is not near gravel or the bacterial colonies in the gravel, so important for this method of filtration, will be affected.

Aquarists using the clinical method may install the reactor as a permanent fixture in the tank, but I personally prefer to use it in a quarantine tank along with other medicinal preparations as an aid to healing stricken fishes.

The ultra-violet steriliser

Another expensive piece of equipment which, when used in the correct manner, can also prove beneficial to marine fishes. By its design it allows water to be pumped around an ultra-violet lamp, which has the effect of sterilising the water by killing the protozoa and bacteria as it passes through the outer tube. Again, this is primarily used in the clinical tank.

Water

There are several excellent prepared sea-salt mixes on the market at the moment; most of which are of a very high quality. I would advise buying them rather than all the separate chemical ingredients and mixing it yourself, because unless the aquarist requires a considerable amount it is not economical.

Before mixing the salt water refer to the individual manufacturer's instructions, but as a rough guide the procedure is as follows: a large—preferably plastic—container should be used and this is filled with fresh water; then, *all* the salt mixture is tipped into this and stirred vigorously until the chemicals have been dissolved and the liquid is reasonably clear. Next, if any sachets or bottles of liquid ingredients are included in the manufacturer's mixture these should be added. This concentrated solution can then be poured into the tank and topped up with more fresh water to about three-fifths of the level required. (A tip to follow: if a bowl is placed in the tank first and then water is poured slowly into it, so as to trickle gently over the sides, then the force of water will not disturb the gravel or any other aquarium decoration in the process.)

When the tank is three-fifths full, decoration can be carried out with suitable rocks and corals. (The reason for not filling the tank completely before adding the coral and rocks is that the water displaced by these would overflow.) After this has been completed, the heater and air-pump can be switched on and the tank topped up. Finally, ensure that the specific gravity reading of the water is correct.

Shells

Besides being an attractive form of decoration and a means of refuge for small or timid fish, shells perform an important stabilising task when they are included in a marine set-up. Because of their calcium content they act as a chemical buffer, helping to keep the water reading well into the alkaline side of the pH scale.

The pictures that follow show some of the shells that may be used, but care should be exercised when preparing them for the tank. They must be soaked thoroughly in water for twenty-four hours and then rinsed and shaken until all signs of their previous occupants have been removed and they are quite clean.

Chiragra (*Lambis sp*)

Pink or Queen Conch (*Strombus gigas*)

Rose Murex (*Murex erythrestomus*)

Orange Spider (*Lambis crocata*)

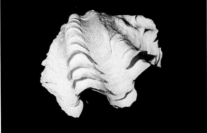

Frilly Clam (*Tridacna sp*)

Common Murex

Rose Green Abalone (*Haliotidae sp*)

Tiger Cowrie (*Cypraea tigris*)

Melon Shell

Bull Mouth Helmet (*Cypraecassis rufa*)

Bursa Frog Shell (*Bursa bufo*)

Yellow Helmet

23

Specific gravity and the hydrometer

If the density of pure water at 39°F (4°C) is 1 gram per cubic centimeter, then the specific gravity of an equal volume of sea water will be 1·023 times heavier. This applies to any substance, be it acid or alkali, providing the comparison is made when both substances are at the same temperature.

The table below shows how the variations in the specific gravity of a substance are not only dependent on density but also on temperature.

°C	Specific gravity			
20	1·0200	1·0215	1·0231	1·0259
21	1·0198	1·0214	1·0229	1·0258
22	1·0197	1·0212	1·0227	1·0256
23	1·0195	1·0210	1·0224	1·0254
24	1·0193	1·0207	1·0222	1·0252
25	1·0190	1·0205	1·0220	1·0250
26	1·0187	1·0202	1·0217	1·0247
27	1·0184	1·0199	1·0213	1·0243

Temperature in °C

Fortunately, special hydrometers are available for the marine aquarist which will measure the specific gravity of sea water at the temperature level required in a tropical marine tank. These are obtainable from most dealers who stock marine fish.

The hydrometer is not unlike a fisherman's float in shape and is weighted internally so that when floating a reading can be taken from the point along the stem which is level with the surface of the water—this tells you the specific gravity of the water.

A hydrometer must be used when mixing sea water. If it reads higher than 1·020–1·023, as it will during the initial mixing, then the sea water should be diluted carefully with fresh water to bring it to the correct reading. Allow time for the water and salt to become thoroughly mixed before taking a final reading.

pH value

In layman's terms, the pH value is a way of describing the acid or alkali content of a liquid. The pH scale is graded between 0 and 14, where 0 is the strongest degree of acidity and 14 is the strongest degree of alkalinity. Therefore 7, being mid-scale, is neutral. A pH of 8·2–8·4 is ideal for a marine tank.

As can be seen from the diagram, pure water will give a reading of 7·0; water from an area rich in peat will give a reading on the acid side of the pH scale, whereas water from a chalk or limestone district will have a high alkali content.

Tap water varies from place to place and can read from 6·6 to 7·4. However, this does not have a great bearing on the final pH reading of sea water, once mixed, because all commercially prepared mixtures are designed to produce a reading of around 8·3.

The aquarist is advised to purchase a saltwater pH kit. This will enable him to maintain the correct pH level in his tank.

This is usually done by taking a sample, adding a measured amount of the reagent and comparing the colour result with the colours on the chart provided. Somewhat similar, in fact, to the procedure used with the nitrite test kits.

The pH of sea water does not vary a great deal, but if it does this usually indicates that all is not well with some other aspect of the water under test.

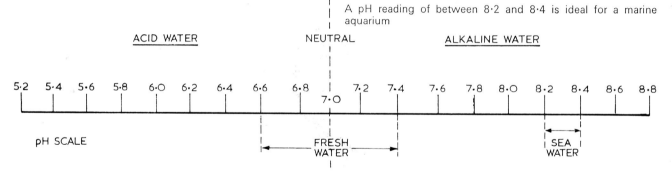

A pH reading of between 8·2 and 8·4 is ideal for a marine aquarium

The alkali reserve and the use of pH buffers and adjusters

The alkali reserve kit is designed to be used at a pH of 8·2–8·3 and will monitor the water conditions in the tank. The importance of maintaining a high level of alkalinity reserve and therefore buffering capacity in sea water has been well known for several years. Failure to do so can result in a sharp and possibly lethal drop in the pH value. Rectification of the alkali reserve can be done by the careful use of buffering solutions on a weekly basis.

Regular addition of buffering solutions can be excellent for the maintenance of high quality marine aquarium water, but there are occasions when the pH can drop drastically despite a high level of alkali reserve.

In these cases no amount of additional buffers or adjusters will rectify the situation and other causes must be sought.

Among the major causes of a fall in pH value where the alkali reserve is still quite high are:

A dead fish or invertebrate rotting away unseen

Over-stocking with fish and/or invertebrates

Lack of adequate algal growth to maintain the correct water chemistry

pH and alkali reserve test kits are essential aids to good water management, since they enable the marine aquarist to keep an up-to-date check on the exact water conditions.

There are several good brands of test kits on the market. These have been tried and tested as to their effectiveness and it is a good idea to pay a visit to your local fish-dealer. He has the most up-to-date information available and will be able to explain how to test the water, the way a particular test kit is used, and often recommend the most reliable one.

All water test kits do, however, have very explicit instructions as to their use.

Aquarium decoration

Organ Pipe Coral (*Tubipora musica*)

Corals

The keeping and culturing of living corals should not be attempted until the tank has had a chance to mature, so that the coral polyps can derive some nutrition from the suspended matter in the water.

It takes a correctly set-up marine bio-system plus an experienced aquarist to enable successful growth of coral in a tank. Once it has been established, though, the result is literally a coral reef in one's living room.

A point that should not be overlooked is that a great number of marine fishes spend most of their time feeding on coral-forming polyps. Therefore it goes without saying that these fishes should not be included in such a bio-system. Indeed, skeletons of dead coral as illustrated here can provide an attractive method of aquarium decoration.

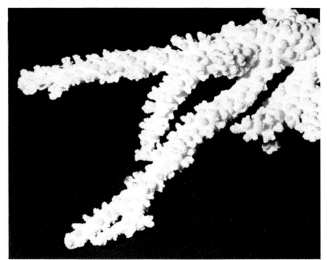
Branch Coral (*Acropora arcuata*)

Blue or Fire Coral (*Heliopora caerulea*)

(above) Caulerpa sertularoides; (below) C. crassifolia (see page 30)

It seems unbelievable that tiny creatures like the coral polyps can produce such beautiful underwater gardens, but they do, and a coral flower is one of nature's wonders. Through the ages, coral has been much revered and men earn their living collecting it.

It is formed over a period of time by the calcereous skeletal deposits of the dead polyps. Obviously, the species of polyp determines what form and colour the coral head takes. There are many types of coral heads and in the sea they are brightly coloured, but once they are brought to the surface and dried they lose their colour and most types turn white. In fact the only true brightly coloured coral is the Red Organ Pipe. Their loss of colour does not detract from their beauty, though, and in this form they are now accepted as an aid to producing realism in a marine aquarium.

Coral cleaning

Before placing coral in an aquarium it should be well cleaned and inspected. This is because due to its structure minute creatures find that it makes an ideal refuge for them and so become lodged in it and die. Therefore, until all the previous occupants have been removed it cannot be effectively utilised. This is not an easy task and cleaning it can take quite a while. There are two methods of achieving this:

Method 1

First boil the coral in fresh water for one hour. Then spray with cold water from a hose to remove as many loose particles as possible. After this stand it in a bucket of water overnight and hose it down again the following day. Finally, leave it out in the sun to bleach for two or three days. (For dense varieties, such as Brain coral, this method should be repeated.)

Method 2

Stand the coral in a bucket of mild bleach solution for twenty-four hours, then remove and rinse well until the smell of bleach has disappeared completely.

With this method, removal of the smell of bleach can prove to be almost as big a problem as the one which it was designed to eliminate.

Brain Coral (*Diploria cerebriformis*)

Thorny Coral (*Pocillopora damicornis*)

Finger Coral (*Acropora humilis*)

Mushroom Coral (*Fungia fungites*)

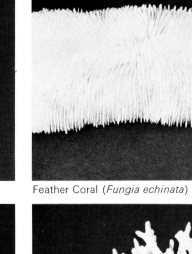
Feather Coral (*Fungia echinata*)

Figured Coral (*Merulina ampliata*)

Birds Nest Coral (*Seriatopora sp*)

Brown Stem Coral (*Acropora sanguinolenta*)

Cluster Coral (*Acropora sp*)

29

Commercial coral cleaners can also be bought, although by choice I have not used them.

Once cleaned it can be arranged in the tank to provide refuge for the fishes and if done artistically it will enhance the overall effect of the marine aquarium.

Plants

Of the higher forms of plants available for the aquarium, *Caulerpa* (usually *C. prolifera*) is most often seen. Although it is not particularly hardy it is most suited to aquarium life, and in order to get the best results *C. prolifera* must be purchased still attached to its original anchoring points. These are often small pieces of rock chipped off along with plants to avoid damaging the root structure.

Once established in a tank a certain amount of care is still required in order to keep the plants healthy. Any dead or discoloured leaves must be removed as these will affect the water chemistry. Plant foods such as algae fertilisers may be used to provide nutrition, although a check should be made to establish whether or not the fertiliser in use is suitable for salt water. Most commercial preparations have it marked on the wrapper. However, this is of academic interest to the beginner, since he should not attempt to keep the higher plant life until a considerable amount of general experience has been gained.

Lower forms of plant life, such as the algae that form a light carpet over most objects in a tank, are much easier to establish, and with a little knowledge the aquarist can produce them in various colour forms. Once again careful use of fertilisers and regulated amounts of light will soon produce brown, blue and even red algae. This latter, though not often seen, is highly prized by most aquarists.

Other types of aquarium decoration

Because of the difficulty involved in keeping marine plants healthy in an aquarium the beginner will have to settle for the next best thing. I have already mentioned corals as a form of decoration, but the following items may assist the newcomer in adding a touch of realistic beauty to his tank.

Rockwork

This can be helpful in lending a natural look to a tank. The artistic aquarist can create charming caves and grottos which the fish will love. It is important, however, that the rocks be chosen with care. Those that have a metal content should not be included, nor those that are porous or liable to break up in salt water. Sandstone, Westmorland and Devon black stone can be used, as can certain types of volcanic lava. Fused glass rocks are a good stand-by and look quite attractive once they are established and have a coat of algae covering them.

The cleaning of rocks is quite easy, since the majority only require a good scrubbing under a cold water tap. But any rocks of a doubtful origin should be boiled in a pan of water for twenty minutes to make sure they are absolutely clean.

It is a good idea to try and match the rocks when several are used in the same aquarium. By this I mean using only one type of rock per tank. This is especially effective if the rocks are so arranged that the strata run all the same way. Using this method avoids the impression of them being just thrown in the tank.

Above right: The yawning phenomenon (see page 32)
Right: The most frequently seen symbiotic relationship in an aquarium is the Clownfish/Anemone partnership

Care and maintenance

About marine fishes

Though not as advanced in the evolutionary process as the human being, fish do have a biological complexity which must be understood before any success in keeping them in captivity is to be expected. In this short chapter an attempt has been made to allow the potential aquarist to familiarise himself with the various aspects of marine fish-keeping in general.

Biology

Below is a diagram of a fish which has been labelled to illustrate more clearly various points on the body. These terms are widely accepted by marine biologists and ichthyologists and it is a good idea to become familiar with this nomenclature when referring to the fishes.

Osmosis

This is the term used to describe what happens when a semi-permeable membrane, in this case the skin tissue of a fish, separates a low-concentration solution from a high-concentration solution, a movement of water molecules taking place through that membrane from the former solution to the latter.

In the case of a salt-water fish there is always a tendency for it to lose body fluid into its surrounding environment. Therefore, to counteract this, it must continually 'drink' sea water. The salt is excreted either through the kidney or with the aid of salt-secreting cells in the gill filaments. Occasionally a fish may be seen to 'yawn' and this phenomenon has been attributed to the fact that excess salts build up in the gill filaments, therefore it creates a backwash, rapidly expelling the salt by this 'yawning' action.

It can be seen from this then that any large change in the concentration of salt water in an aquarium will place a strain on the metabolic process of the tank inhabitants to the extent that they may die as a result of this change.

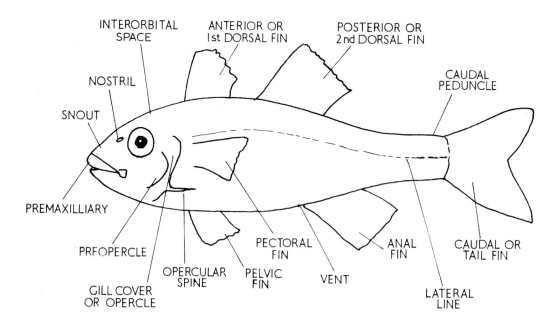

Symbiosis

If two different kinds of animals are found living together the association is said to be symbiotic. Furthermore, if one of the animals benefits from this association it is termed commensalism. If both of them benefit then we call this mutualism.

The most frequently seen form of symbiosis in an aquarium is the clownfish/anemone partnership. In this case the clownfish is able to live amongst the poisonous tentacles of an anemone with complete impunity. It does this by gradually coating itself with a mucous substance that the anemone produces to protect against self-stinging. This is not the only example of symbiosis that is encountered in aquariums, but it is the most common. Other examples include the associations between anemones and shrimps and between anemones and hermit crabs. Probably the best known symbiotic relationship of marine creatures is that between remoras and sharks.

Cleaning activities

There are many species of fishes and invertebrates in the sea which perform a form of cleaning service. For instance, a Cleaner Wrasse (*Labroides dimidiatus*) or a Banded Coral Shrimp (*Stenopus hispidus*) will 'set-up shop' near a convenient coral head or clump of rock and proceed to thoroughly clean fishes by picking at parasites on the fishes body. They may even enter the gills and mouth of a large predator in order to perform a better service, but almost always come to no harm. Most fishes accept this as part of the normal life on a reef and in some cases will form queues at a 'cleaning station', waiting patiently whilst the cleaner busies itself with other members of the shoal.

A Red-lined Shrimp (*Lysmata grabhami*) is seen here performing a cleaning service on a Coral Beauty (*Centropyge bispinosus*) in one of the author's tanks

Tank servicing

Once a tank is set up it requires constant attention. Unlike an aquarium with undergravel filtration, a clinical aquarium cannot be left for long periods without a complete water change. The best method is to replace one gallon (4·5 litres) per month; after six months to change half of the water; then after one year to do a complete tank service and water change.

Before beginning on this job a temporary tank will be required in which to house the fishes whilst maintenance is being carried out. It can be filled with some of the old water for this purpose. When netting the fish, all corals and rocks should be removed to make the operation easier and also to ensure that the fish do not damage themselves whilst fleeing from the net. Once this is done the tank should be drained and the coral, rocks and gravel scrubbed until they look like new. The tank can then be cleaned and filled with freshly prepared water. Remember to ensure that the corals and rocks are returned to their original positions; this prevents territorial squabbles when the fish are returned to the tank.

Once the tank is filled the water should be well aerated before replacing the inmates, checking to make sure the temperature and specific gravity are more or less equal to that of the old water.

If undergravel filtration is used a partial water change every six months or so is sufficient. The tank should *never* be completely cleaned out, nor the gravel washed, as this will destroy the precious bacteria colonies present in the tank and the filter will cease to function correctly.

Routine maintenance

It is a good idea to run a check on pH and specific gravity twice weekly and, if an outside filter is used, the filter medium should be changed every one to two weeks.

Any uneaten food is undesirable in a tank. This is one of the prime contributory factors in creating toxic conditions and it should therefore be removed daily with a dip tube or siphon.

A routine check on the condition of the fish themselves should be made daily. If any dead fish are present they should be removed, for a dead fish left in a tank overnight can pollute the water by morning.

A considerable amount of water can be lost through evaporation, and although only pure water is lost into the surrounding atmosphere a certain amount of salt in crystal form is lost due to crusting on the tank frame, filter pipes and cover glass. Therefore a tank cannot be topped up with fresh water indefinitely to compensate for loss through evaporation. It is because of this that a constant check on specific gravity is required.

To sum up: a salt-water tank can be made to run smoothly, providing a little care is taken to ensure that the conditions do not deteriorate too much. After all, the time spent on maintenance—probably only an hour a week is necessary—is a very small price to pay for keeping the fish happy and healthy.

Foods and feeding

The best method of feeding marine fish is to give them little and often; but never put more food in a tank than the fish can eat in two or three minutes. Fishes in their natural habitat are always on the look-out for food, so the greater the number of feedings per day the better. Any surplus food must always be removed.

A wide variety of foods is available to aquarists for feeding to marine fish. The most practical and beneficial foods are:

Mysus shrimp	Mussel	Cockles
Boiled shrimp	Crab	Brine shrimp
Tubifex	Razor meat	Silverfish
Bloodworm	White fish	Algae
Chopped lettuce	Squid	Chopped clam

Occasionally it may be necessary to teach a newly acquired fish to feed. This can usually be done by feeding newly-hatched brine shrimp, for seldom can any fish resist this delicacy. When fish are sold in an emaciated condition, like the one illustrated here, there is very little the aquarist can do to save the life of the fish. So he would be well advised to avoid purchasing specimens like this. It is always a good idea to see that a fish is feeding before buying it.

It must be pointed out at this stage that certain fish require certain foods. Tangs and Surgeonfishes consume great amounts of algae in their natural element, therefore this should be provided whenever they are kept in an aquarium. If no algae is present then chopped lettuce can be substituted.

Live *tubifex* and *daphnia* are of little or no use in a marine tank as they seldom live for more than a few seconds in sea water; there is also the possibility that disease can be introduced with these foods.

Freeze-dried and flake foods provide a good staple diet for quite a lot of fish, but some form of live food should be included at regular intervals.

Feeding invertebrates can often be a tricky problem—particularly the filter feeding ones, for which liquid fry food is a good standby. A crushed prawn head placed near a piece of living coral is another good recipe.

For the larger invertebrates, such as sea anemones, lobsters or large starfish, the problem is less difficult. Occasionally an anemone may kill and eat a fish, (see photograph overleaf), but this is very rare and usually only happens when the fish is ill anyway. Anemones should be fed about twice a week with a small cube of prawn or shrimp, though if this is refused squid or mussel may be tried.

Frozen foods are by far the most important for the marine aquarist. Nowadays the choice is varied and most fish-dealers can offer a range of frozen squid, mussel, crab, shrimp, clam, cockles, razor meat, etc. Often pre-packed, it can be stored in a freezer compartment of a refrigerator or deep-freeze for weeks on end, and used at will. It is often 'gamma irradiated' thereby reducing the chances of disease being transmitted to the aquarium from the food itself. Most modern pre-packages are frozen relatively flat in order that daily portions may easily be broken off.

Above right and centre: Platax tiera and Arusetta asfur being fed flake food by hand in one of the authors aquaria
Right: A tank set-up using under-gravel filtration

Above: A rare sight in an aquarium : the Squirrelfish was dying,
but the Anemone made sure of it, while the Clownfish,
which has a symbiotic relationship with the Anemone,
appears unconcerned

Opposite above: Feeding time in the author's aquarium
Opposite below: An emaciated Triggerfish

Quarantine

There is always a problem when adding new fishes to an already established system because disease on a new arrival may be passed on to the rest of the tank occupants. Often this results in serious losses. By observing a few simple rules, however, the aquarist can minimise this possibility.

When the new fish is brought home it should be kept at first in a smaller separate tank provided with suitable rocks and coral in which to hide, for it will almost certainly be suffering from shock during the first few hours. This is called a quarantine tank. It has the main advantage that if disease does become apparent it can be treated without any danger to other tank occupants such as delicate corals or anemones. The new arrival should be kept in quarantine for a period of two weeks or until all traces of a previous disease have been eliminated.

Sometimes it is not practical or too costly for the aquarist to set up an additional aquarium for the sole purpose of quarantine. In this case there is another solution. When a new fish is purchased, it can be paid for but left in the dealer's tank and observed for the same period. I have found that reputable dealers are most happy to oblige.

Copper-based cures

Care should be taken when using all copper-based cures, since they are deadly to most forms of invertebrate life. Never, therefore, quarantine the fish in a tank which contains any invertebrates. Moreover, the manufacturers' instructions should be followed closely, since an excess amount of copper in the water can kill even the fish.

Disease guide

For reference I have included a quick guide to the most common diseases that are liable to crop up. It is by no means comprehensive, but it will help in the speedy diagnosis and cure of the more usual ailments. By experience I have found the cures stated to be the most effective.

It has to be admitted that the aquarist may have to deal with fish ailments fairly frequently, which is unfortunate but sometimes unavoidable. Nearly always the problem can be cut down to a bare minimum if specimens are properly quarantined before they are introduced with other fish.

Disease guide

Disease	Description	Symptom	Cure
Oodinium	Parasitic, attacking the gills and body of a fish. Initially causing irritation and subsequently respiratory failure. Very contagious	Loss of appetite, sluggish movements. Rusty flecks on the body and fins. Fast gill-beat, loss of equilibrium and finally death	Cuprazin or similar copper-based cure
Ichthyophonus	An internal parasite developing into a fungus. May be caused through feeding contaminated foods	Belly swollen and inflamed. Scales sticking out from the body as the disease takes hold	Isolate and treat with antibiotics. The use of ozone sometimes proves beneficial

Lymphocystis	A virus, not always fatal but nevertheless contagious, affecting the fish Chelmon rostratus in particular	One or more cysts, cream in colour, between 1–2mm in diameter on the sides and head of the fish	Isolate the affected fish and let the disease run its course. The alternative is to cut the cyst out and treat the wound with methylene blue
Cryptocaryon irritans	Known to freshwater aquarists as 'Ich'. It is a virulent parasite which attacks the skin and gills of a fish causing difficulty in breathing and sometimes death	Loss of appetite and increased respiratory movement. A dusting of tiny white spots on the body and fins	Raise the aquarium temperature to 80°F (26°C). Leave lights on and treat with copper as for Oodinium
Benedenia	An external parasite affecting the eyes and gills. It is quite contagious	The fish swim about with fins folded and flick themselves off nearby objects. The eyes cloud over and swell up	Copper treatment such as Cuprazin is effective. Raise the temperature and leave the filter running. Repeat after one week if needed
Fin rot	As the name implies this disease attacks the fin membranes and can affect a whole tank of fish if not checked	The rotting of a fin or part of a fin; fish swimming about in a 'poorly' state	Paint with methylene blue and quarantine for one week, or until cured
Monogenia	Parasitic, attacking the skin and gills. A killer disease in several forms	Increase in respiratory movement. Scratching of the affected area	Examination of the gills should reveal what look like specks of dust; these are the parasites. The affected fish should be quarantined and treated with a mild solution of formalin or a commercial cure
Poisoning	Not a disease but an ailment due to chemical or biological contamination. Fatal if the fish are left in a contaminated environment	Increase in respiratory movement, loss of balance and, in severe cases, poison burns on the body	Remove the affected fishes to a fresh tank with freshly-prepared sea water. Some of the fish can be expected to die
Shock	Again, not a disease but a common occurrence among newly introduced fishes. It can be fatal	Increase in gill-beats per minute. Fish skulk in corners with fins folded. Loss of colour. Dash about wildly when disturbed	Quarantine and try to disturb as little as possible. Provide a hiding place for the fish and keep the tank lights off as much as possible

Breeding marine fishes

Very little has been written on the subject of breeding marine fishes for the simple reason that until now little has been known about this absorbing subject.

It is certainly possible, but not easy, to breed certain species of fishes in a life support system. In reality the problem is not in getting the fish to breed, ie court and lay eggs, but to raise the young *and have them flourish!*

Many species of marine fishes will breed given the right tank conditions without further prompting: this applies particularly to the Demoiselles. Raising the fry into adult fish is unfortunately a different matter and this will be dealt with later on in this chapter.

The parents

Most tropical marine fish are very difficult to sex. With many it is impossible unless the belly is slit open and an examination of the gonads made. Obviously then, since this is impractical for breeding purposes, the potential fish breeder must make do with the sparse information available on those species that can be sexed. Experienced fish handlers—like the staff at a zoo aquarium or a marine research station—are able to successfully determine the sexes of many marine fishes and will freely give advice and help on this subject. As a rule of thumb, though, any two fish that detach themselves from a shoal or group of the same species and establish their own little territory, reacting as a breeding pair, should be assumed to be just that! Adequate conditions may then be provided in order to allow this natural pairing and process of reproduction to go on uninterrupted.

Preparation

If, as is often the case, two fish decide to mate in a community tank then there are two courses open to the aquarist: he can take his chances on them not being too disturbed and remove the pair to another tank; or he can remove the other tank inhabitants. The latter alternative is usually the better proposition. Often a mating pair appear quite unmoved by their close proximity with other fishes, though this is not always the case.

After mating, further choices present themselves: should the eggs be removed, or the parents, or should they both be left to their own devices? Unfortunately, as with everything concerned with aquarium fishes, there is no hard and fast rule.

To prepare a tank specifically for breeding purposes the aquarist should have prior knowledge of the behaviour and breeding pattern of whichever species he intends to propogate. For instance, if he intends to breed and raise Clownfish from a mated pair then his chance of success will be greatly increased if a suitable anemone is present in the prepared tank. Or, as a further example, *Lactoria cornuta*, whose eggs are large and buoyant, would require a tank free of any other fishes which would normally make short work of the eggs.

Temperature is another factor to be taken into consideration when attempting to breed marine fishes since, by carefully raising the temperature of the tank, it is possible to induce the parent fish to lay their eggs. Thus, by maintaining this temperature over the whole breeding season it is possible that the fish may lay eggs several times. Similarly, by lowering the temperature it is possible to create a conditioning season during which the fish are allowed to rest and recover for the next breeding period. The particular temperature at which the fish are bred is not as important as how much it is raised for the breeding cycle (this would normally mean raising 72 °F to 76 °F [22 °C to 25·5 °C] or 75 °F to 79 °F [24 °C to 26 °C]). It can be seen then that, because of the lack of hard and fast rules, the potential marine fish breeder must remain flexible in his approach to obtain satisfactory results.

Above and below. Typical behavioural postures exhibited by a pair of *Amphiprion ephippium* prior to spawning in a community tank.

Spawning

As has been previously stated, the eggs may be buoyant or even negatively buoyant (ie they may sink to the bottom). Usually the eggs are laid in several strings of up to sixty eggs each on a rock or solid piece of substrate. At this stage the eggs are vulnerable to all sorts of dangers, including predacean, fungusing or merely being sucked up a filter pipe. In order to protect them from this sort of danger the aquarist must have taken steps during the initial setting-up to guard against this eventuality. Fungusing of eggs, however, is quite difficult to eradicate, particularly with the eggs of the Pomacentrids. This danger can be reduced considerably, though, if an air-stone is placed near the eggs so that the bubbles gently wash over them during the incubation period. If the parents are left in with the eggs then this will not apply because any eggs which do fungus will usually be picked out and eaten by the parent fish.

Marine fishes normally make pretty attentive parents during the initial incubation period. This is particularly the case with the Cardinal-fishes (*Apogonidae*) which are essentially 'mouth brooders'. This means that the eggs are incubated in the mouth of one of the parent fish in the same way that some freshwater Cichlids do. With Sea Horses it is the male which incubates the young in a brood pouch after which they are expelled as live young.

Hatching

The length of incubation and subsequent hatching of eggs varies from species to species. Usually the hatching occurs at night. At this stage the new-born fry are equipped with a yolk-sac which is used up in a very short time. It is therefore important to start feeding the fry as soon as possible. Most species are pelagic at this point, though after a short time they may settle to the bottom and relative safety.

Rearing

Correct food plays a vital part at this stage in the frys' life and, though many have tried, no universally accepted marine fry food has been produced. One concoction, comprising of a mixture of shrimp, mussel, crab, silkworm pupa, dried cod-liver oil, wheatgerm, fish blood, sea-weed, bone-meal, feed lime, sea water, egg yolk, curds, horsemeat, ant pupa and water soluble chlorophyll, as well as vitamins and antibiotics, has been tried with seemingly successful results (Hackinger: 'Anemonefishes reared in the aquarium', *Aquarien Magazine*, 1967). For the mere hobbyist, though, this strained pulp would be too impractical and expensive to produce. So we must experiment with various food forms such as natural plankton which could, in itself, prove to be the only solution to the problem. As has always been the case the aquarist, having bred his fish, must be prepared to lose a proportion of his fry. This is not so bad really when one considers that many fish, having produced eggs in an aquarium once, may spawn again at regular intervals throughout the breeding season. This offers an ideal opportunity to try new food variants. Often liquid fry food—normally only used for fresh-water fishes and filter-feeding invertebrates—is a good standby, though it is doubtful whether this alone is enough for the young fry to obtain sufficient nutrients. It may, however, be blended with brine shrimp nauplii and then dispersed with a pipette, a little at a time, into the fry tank. A point to remember with young fishes is that they need feeding every few hours or so during

Nest caring activity of *Amphiprion frenatus* at SeAquariums Waterlife Research Ltd. Photograph by Graham Cox

the first few days; later they should be of sufficient size to take newly hatched brine shrimp or finely ground shrimp and mussel flesh.

Recommended fishes for the inexperienced breeder

It is true to say that most aquarists are inexperienced at breeding fishes since very little has been published on this subject. From my own experiences, I would recommend the following families as being the most likely candidates for the aquarist who wants to try his hand at breeding:

Apogonidae	the Cardinalfishes
Blenniidae	the Blennies
Gobiidae	the Gobies
Serranidae	mainly the Hamlets
Ostraciidae	*Lactoria cornuta* in particular
Pomacanthidae	principally the genus *Centropyge*
Pomacentridae	Demoiselles and Anemonefishes
Sciaenidae	genus *Equetus*
Syngnathidae	Sea Horses and Pipefishes

Peacock Blenny (*Blennius pavo*) which can be bred by the inexperienced aquarist

Above: Juvenile Bowtie Damsel or Blue Fin Damsel (*Paragly-phidodon melanopus*)

Opposite: Cardinalfish sheltering amongst a Sea Urchin's spines
Photo : Bruce Coleman

First aid kit

Every marine aquarist should have his own first aid kit for emergencies, which should contain the following items:

    Tweezers
    Scissors
    Quarantine net (for sick fish only)
    Solution of potassium permanganate
    Solution of copper sulphate
    Small plastic dish
    Spare salt pack (for emergency water change)

Fish facts

The approximate lifespan is 3 to 5 years. In general terms, sexual maturity is reached at 12 to 18 months, but earlier in some species. There is enormous variation in rates of growth, from 1 inch per month in the case of Batfishes to 1 inch per year in the case of Demoiselles. When assessing the size of your aquarium, a basic rule of thumb to apply is 1 gallon of water per inch of fish. The sizes given are for fully grown adult fishes unless otherwise stated.

All the fishes photographed in colour are live specimens with the exception of the following which proved difficult to obtain: Lemon Butterflyfish (*Chaetodon miliaris*), Palau Squirrelfish (*Adioryx tiere*), Blue Fin or Banana Wrasse (*Thallasoma lutescens*) and Stripey (*Microcanthus strigatus*).

Zanclus, Moorish Idol or Toby (*Zanclus canescens*)

Opposite: Scorpionfish (*Pterois lunulata*)

Part 2 Coral Fishes

This section of the book is set out in family order;
each family is split up into different genera, the genera
being listed in alphabetical order for ease of reference.
Where families are very closely related these have been
combined. An introduction is included at the
beginning of each particular group of fishes,
containing additional information which is common
to that family.

The use of latin names for the various species is, at
best, open to criticism. In recent years it has become
almost a pastime for Ichthyologists to change the
name of a fish with ensuing confusion amongst
hobbyists. In many respects this is a good thing
because out of this controversy should come
increased knowledge.

The author has no wish to use this book as a platform
on which to base arguments for or against the use of
a particular latin name but rather as a guide to a
selection of fishes chosen primarily for their
availability and suitability for a marine aquarium
in the home.

See page 145 for a complete list of coral fishes illustrated in Part 2

Opposite: Three Butterflyfishes, *Chaetodon aurega, C. Chrysurus* and *C. Trifasciatus*
Photo : Bruce Coleman

Acanthuridae (Surgeons and Tangs)

Including the following genera:

Acanthurus	Paracanthurus
Ctenochaetus	Zebrasoma
Naso	

Distributed throughout the warm seas of the world, this family is comprised of active swimmers which have a tendency to shoal. They are vegetarians with small mouths. One of the outstanding characteristics of these fishes is the scalpel on each side of the caudal peduncle which is used as a weapon and is very sharp. Normally these knife-like appendages are folded flat against the body, but when annoyed the fish raises them, and with a flick of the tail can cause serious damage to another fish.

In an aquarium, however, they are normally peaceful, providing they are not kept with other big fish. Their tank should be rather warmer than usual (80°F or 26·5°C at least). Whilst being rather hard to keep, if there is plenty of space and algae they should not present too much of a problem to the experienced aquarist. Most species swim with pectoral fins only and tend to lose some of their colour with age. When handling these fishes, great care should be taken as some species have poisonous dorsal and anal spines, particularly when young. The principal genera are *Acanthurus* and *Zebrasoma*.

Popular name: **Achilles Tang** or **Red-tailed Surgeon**
Size: 10in (250mm)
Distribution: Pacific Ocean from Hawaii to the Philippines and China

This is a typical reef fish which is frequently seen in large shoals in its natural habitat. The juveniles are sombre in colour, displaying none of the brilliant red markings which develop as they reach adulthood.

Aquarium specimens need special care: plenty of well-oxygenated water in which to swim and a liberal supply of freeze-dried or fresh protein supplemented with algae. If a plentiful supply of algae is not present well washed lettuce leaves tied to a piece of string and suspended in the tank will suffice to replace this deficiency. (The string enables any uneaten food to be easily removed after feeding.)

Acanthurus achilles (Shaw)

Popular name: **Striped Surgeon**
Size: 12in (300mm)
Distribution: Indo-Pacific

Sometimes called the Majestic Surgeonfish, this species is not as colourful as the above fish. It grows quite large, is a most hardy species and will usually rule the roost wherever it is kept. This should not deter the aquarist, provided that he has a large enough tank. Personally, I have found this species rather too boisterous.

A. bleekeri is quite rare in its natural environment and therefore not easy to obtain.

Acanthurus bleekeri (Günther)

Popular name: **Blue Tang**
Size: 10in (250mm)
Distribution: Tropical Atlantic

The feeding pattern of this fish is typical of its family, requiring plenty of green matter in its diet. Startling colour changes affect this species. The young fish are yellow with blue in the eyes and on the tip of the dorsal fin. As it passes from the juvenile stage the yellow base colouration becomes less distinct and is replaced by a pattern of horizontal lines on the sides. The blue tips to the dorsal and anal fins also become more apparent. The adult retains only a trace of yellow in the fins and tail.

Due to this drastic colour variation, it is not uncommon for the young to be confused with *Zebrasoma flavascens* and the adults with *A. bleekeri.*

If a juvenile is purchased, and they are not rare, then this colour change can be observed over a period of about 18 months.

above: juvenile
left: sub-adult

Acanthurus coeruleus (Bloch & Schneider)

Popular name: **Powder-Brown Tang** or **Golden-rimmed Surgeon**
Size: 7in (180mm)
Distribution: Indo-Pacific, from the tropical islands of the East Pacific to Cocos Keeling Island in the East Indian Ocean

Aquarium life seems to suit this fish more than most members of this family. It is a boisterous character that will usually take over any community tank and become quite territorial. It will not tolerate the presence of another member of its family.

The young fish is not so colourful as the adult, which has a splendid livery rich in colour. Feeding may be a problem at first, but after a few days most foods will be accepted. Algae is beneficial so the wise aquarist will ensure that a plentiful supply is incorporated in its diet.

Acanthurus glaucopareius (Cuvier)

Popular name: **Powder Blue Surgeon**
Size: 10in (250mm)
Distribution: East Africa to the East Indies

A very striking fish that is unmistakable once
seen. It is popular among marine aquarists but
unfortunately it can sometimes prove to be a
difficult fish. It is very choosy about its food
and consequently I do not advocate it for the
beginner. A prime specimen, however, will eat
a wide variety of foods, from algae or lettuce
to fresh protein, such as frozen brine or fairy
shrimp.

As can be seen from the photograph its colour
is outstanding and in order to have it retain
this optimum tank conditions should be
provided, the most important being plenty of
free swimming space and a large amount of
aeration.

Acanthurus leucosternum (Bennett)

Popular name: **Green-line Surgeon** or
Clown Surgeon
Size: 8in (200mm)
Distribution: Tropical Indo-Pacific

If ever a species was evolved specifically for
showing in public aquaria it must be *A.
lineatus*. It is, in fact, a perfect example of
nature's ability to create colour contrasts with
almost breathtaking results.

It is reasonably undemanding in its food
requirements, but as with others of this genus
it needs plenty of free swimming space.

The body is elongate and compressed laterally,
with a rather large head. The tail is deeply
forked and the markings on it change slightly
as the fish reaches maturity.

Although quite expensive, it is well worth
acquiring. Young specimens are ideal for a
community set-up, but as with most of this
family belligerence increases with age.

Acanthurus lineatus (Linnaeus)

Popular name: **Black Surgeon Fish** or
Grey Surgeon
Size: 16in (400mm)
Distribution: Indo-Pacific

This is a rare fish not often seen in private or
public aquaria, but it is included here because
it will flourish in an aquarium. It has never
become popular with marine aquarists because
of its size and lack of bright body colour.
Nevertheless, if space can be found for one of
these specimens it will do well in a home
aquarium and will grow quite quickly on
tubifex or brine shrimp along with plenty of
green stuff.

Acanthurus gahhm (Forskal)

Naso brevirostris (Valenciennes)

Popular name: **Unicorn Tang** or **Short-nosed Unicorn Tang**
Size: 20in (500mm)
Distribution: Tropical Indo-Pacific

This and the following species are characterised by an unusual protuberance on the forehead, but this is more pronounced in the Unicorn Tang, hence the common name.
The colouration of the two species is similar in the juvenile state, being dark with a sprinkling of white spots and blotches. The mature *N. brevirostris* carries an overall greyish colour and the tail is not forked.
Feeding can present a real problem and if any success is to be achieved with this species the aquarist is advised to buy young specimens which are better able to adapt to aquarium foods supplemented with algae.

Naso lituratus (Bloch & Schneider)

Popular name: **Japanese Tang** or **Smooth-head Unicorn Fish**
Size: 20in (500mm)
Distribution: Indo-Pacific, Red Sea

This species, although much more colourful than the Unicorn Tang, presents the same feeding problems.
The tail is deeply forked due to the elongated top and bottom rays of the caudal fin. Twin scalpels adorn each side of the peduncle and are surrounded by patches of deep orange. This orange colour is also present in the dorsal and anal fins.
Perhaps the most striking feature of this fish, though, is the unusual markings around the head giving it an unmistakable appearance.
It is quite often seen in the shops, being relatively common in its natural environment. However it is never cheap.

Paracanthus theutis (Lacépède)

Popular name: **Regal Tang, Morpho Butterfly** or **Blue Surgeon**
Size: 9in (230mm)
Distribution: Indo-Pacific

Probably this is the most beautifully coloured member of this family and a fish which once seen you will never forget.
Having kept several specimens I have once or twice experienced difficulty in introducing them into an aquarium. However, once having overcome the shock of being scooped up out of familiar surroundings, transported in a bag and let out again into totally unfamiliar surroundings, this species will flourish. It should be remembered that on the reefs this is a shoaling fish which spends a lot of time grazing on the beds of algae. Therefore, an adequate supply of green foodstuff should be included in its diet.

Popular name: Yellow Tang
Size: 6in (150mm)
Distribution: Hawaii, Tropical Indo-Pacific

Specimens which are imported in poor
condition seldom have a chance of survival in
an aquarium, so care should be taken to
choose only the healthiest fish.
A fat and healthy Yellow Tang can most easily
be induced to feed on frozen shrimp or mussel
flesh. Tubifex and brine shrimp are also good
stand-bys for more difficult fish. They need
plenty of green stuff and a well matured tank
is required if they are to be kept with any
degree of success.
Regarding tank conditions, to me the best
parameters are: pH 8·2 to 8·3; SG 1·020;
temperature 79°F (26°C).
Although this is definitely not a beginner's fish,
I see no reason why an aquarist with several
months' experience should not keep this fish.

Zebrasoma flavescens (Bennett)

Popular name: Mink Tang or **Brown Tang**
Size: 6in (150mm)
Distribution: Tropical Indo-Pacific

This species is readily available and has
become increasingly popular with aquarists
over the last few years. It is not brightly
coloured but adapts quickly to aquarium life.
Specimens can often be seen in the shops at
less than 1in in length and being so small it
might be assumed that they would have little
chance of survival, but this is not the case;
even at this stage of their lives they are able
to cope with all but the most aggressive tank
mates. Obviously the aquarist would be asking
for trouble if he attempted to keep them with
large predatory species, but within reason it is
safe to house them in a community tank.
Feeding presents no problem, since their diet
does not differ from that of other Tangs.

Zebrasoma scopas (Cuvier)

Popular name: Sailfin Tang
Size: 15in (380mm)
Distribution: Tropical Indo-Pacific

The Sailfin Tang, as it is generally called, is
quite widespread and juveniles often appear
in the shops at quite reasonable prices.
Indian Ocean specimens differ from the
Pacific form in colouration, particularly on the
tail, and ray counts also vary. This has given
rise to the theory that there are two separate
species: Z. veliferum (Pacific) and Z.
desjardinii (Indian Ocean).
Both subspecies are hardy and will live for
quite a long time in a tank. I have found that
they are particularly fond of frozen shrimp and
an occasional helping of spinach. Once their
initial timidness has been overcome they will
even allow themselves to be hand fed.

Zebrasoma veliferum (Bloch)

Comprised of small active fish, this family contains members from most tropical and sub-tropical regions, but they are particularly common in the shallow water of the reefs in the Indo-Pacific area. These fish have stocky bodies and large eyes, but in spite of their body shape they are extremely fast swimmers. All members of the family have two dorsal fins and none of them grow to more than 5in (130mm) in length.

Nocturnal by nature (hence the large eyes), they usually have very healthy appetites and in captivity will accept most foods, but are particularly fond of live food in any form. For defending themselves against attackers some specimens have two anal fin spines.

In an aquarium they should be provided with a place to hide and will then soon settle down.

The females are usually larger than the males and, like certain Cichlids, they are mouthbrooders. It is believed the males fertilise the eggs internally after a show of fins and chasing around has taken place. Spawning occurs after about 48 hours and it is the male that broods the eggs in its mouth.

Apogonidae (Cardinalfish)

Including the following genera:

Apogon	Cheilodipterus
Apogonichthys	Sphaeramia

Sphaeramia nematopterus (Bleeker)

Popular name: **Common Pyjama Cardinal Fish** or **Orbiculate Cardinal Fish**
Size: 3in (80mm)
Distribution: Indo-Pacific

This species of Cardinal Fish is easy to keep and will soon learn to settle down and enjoy living in an aquarium where life is not quite the battle for survival that it is on the reefs or in the open sea.

It is a slow moving fish, and although an occasional specimen will accept dried foods, they generally prefer some form of fresh protein such as shrimp flesh or beef heart. As can be seen from the photograph the body is somewhat curious in shape. The eyes are red and the body is quite deep in relation to its length. As with all Cardinal fishes the tail is forked.

It is hardy and can be included in the list of fishes recommended for beginners.

Popular name: **Mottled Cardinal**
Size: 3in (80mm)
Distribution: Indo-Pacific

This species is often confused with *Sphaeramia nematopterus*. Close inspection shows that the colouration of this fish is much more mundane. It is not a very popular aquarium fish, because of its lack of colour and also because it becomes active only at night. It prefers fresh protein food forms to dried or freeze-dried preparations.

Sphaeramia orbicularis

55

Balistidae (Triggerfish)

Including the following genera:

Amanses	Melichthys
Balistes	Odonus
Balistoides	Pseudobalistes
Balistapus	Rhinecanthus
Hemibalistes	Sufflamen

Perhaps the most outstanding feature common to this family is the unique trigger mechanism. This is a modified first dorsal spine which can be erected and locked into position. Normally the spine fits into a depression on the fish's back, but when danger threatens the fish seeks refuge by wedging itself in a crevice and erecting its spine. When divers go down to catch them they have to release the trigger mechanism before the fish can be extricated. Another feature of this family is the absence of ventral fins, but they have two dorsal fins, the trigger and a posterior soft fin which provides some means of locomotion.

Many Triggerfishes rest in odd positions, such as on their sides or nose-down propped up against a rock.

Found in warm, shallow water of the reefs, these fishes sometimes feed by blowing away the sand to expose food. They are aggressive by nature and some have poisonous flesh. In captivity, however, they make good tank inhabitants, but care should be taken to stay clear of their mouths for they have very powerful jaws and sharp teeth.

Popular name: **Mottled Triggerfish** or **Variegated Trigger**
Size: 6in (150mm)
Distribution: Tropical Indo-Pacific

This little fish is widespread and often seen in dealers' tanks, although never in any great numbers.

It is a hardy little fellow that requires plenty of cover and places to hide. Normally it is relatively slow moving, using its pectoral, dorsal and anal fins to fan its way around the tank. It is capable of sharp bursts of speed, however, and is a master of disguise. In its natural habitat it will disappear into *Sargassum* weed or the like, becoming quite hard to detect. Fresh or frozen shrimp (either adult brine or fairy shrimp) make ideal food for this species. It is used to fresh protein in its natural state and providing this is catered for it will prove a charming inmate for any aquarist lucky enough to obtain one.

Amanses pardalis (Ruppell)

Popular name: **Undulate Triggerfish** or **Orange-green Triggerfish**
Size: 10in (250mm)
Distribution: Indo-Pacific, Hawaii, Red Sea

An attractive addition to a tank, particularly when young. The aquarist should, however, be careful about choosing its tank mates. Although juvenile specimens may not show much aggression, it is as well to be prepared, for as they mature they will exhibit increasing belligerence towards other tank inhabitants. As an aquarium specimen it is attractive, showing an unusual pattern of orange lines, intricately laid on a green base colouration. It is by no means house-proud, though, and will quickly reduce its owner's proudly created coral decor into a pile of rubble. Thankfully, feeding proves less of a dilemma. Most foods are accepted with relish and even flake food can be used, although it is preferable to alternate this with shrimp or mussel flesh.

Balistapus undulatus (Mungo Park)

Balistes bursa (Bloch & Schneider) Photo: Heather Angel

Popular name: **White-lined Triggerfish or Humuhumu Lei** (Hawaiian)
Size: 8in (200mm)
Distribution: Tropical Indo-Pacific, Red Sea

This fish is found in the deeper reaches of the coral reefs, but despite this it is relatively common.
It is similar in colour to *Rhinecanthus aculeatus*, particularly around the large head. The body, though, has a dark patch each side of the vent, and it is this that distinguishes it from other members of this family.
Its hardiness and willingness to feed make it an acceptable aquarium fish. Fresh protein, in any form, is preferred although flake food will be taken to a lesser degree.
(It cannot be stressed enough that a large fish such as this should be provided with ample free-swimming space to ensure a maximum life-span.)

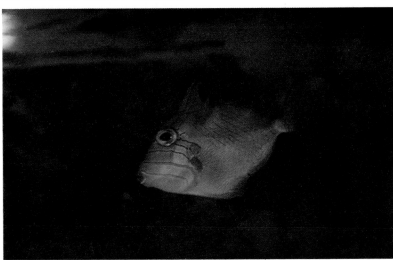

Balistes vetula (Linnaeus)

Popular name: **Queen Triggerfish, Old Wife, Old Wench, Cochino, Peje-puerco**
Size: 15in (380mm)
Distribution: Tropical West Atlantic

Although the young fish are quite attractive, as they reach maturity they undergo a marked change in body shape, becoming almost ugly. Hardly any change in colouration occurs, but the shape of the head, particularly the forehead, takes on an angular appearance. Young specimens are readily available in the shops and it is very seldom one sees mature fish imported.
Fresh or frozen shrimp and mussel flesh are readily acceptable foods—as are small Damsel-fishes, Clownfishes, various invertebrates, and fingers, if the unsuspecting owner is not careful when housing or handling this particular species!

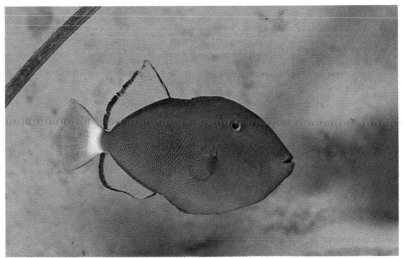

Melichthys vidua (Solander)

Popular name: **Pink-tail Triggerfish**
Size: 11in (280mm)
Distribution: East Indies to Hawaii

This is another good-looking Triggerfish, and once settled in an aquarium it will prove to be quite a character, particularly at feeding time. The body is somewhat sombre in colouration, but this is counter-balanced by creamy-white anal and posterior dorsal fins. These are delicately tipped with black. The bright pink tail is the distinctive feature of this fish.
As is often the case with this family, belligerence increases with age, and this fish is no exception. Feeding, however, presents little difficulty after the fish has overcome the settling in period, and any initial reticence can soon be overcome by tempting it with fresh mussel, clam or crab meat. Once feeding, this specimen will quickly adapt to all the normal aquarium foods.

Popular name : Clown Triggerfish
Size : 18in (450mm)
Distribution : Indo-Pacific to South Africa

Perhaps the best known of the Triggerfish,
this species is often seen in large public
aquaria. Its outstanding colour pattern,
coupled with its adaptability to aquarium life,
make it a popular choice amongst zoos and
fish enthusiasts alike. It is an expensive fish to
buy, but is well worth the money.
It grows quite large and is seldom seen in any
great numbers within its natural habitat.
The bright orange-rimmed mouth contains a
profusion of razor-sharp teeth. Large specimens
should not be kept with other small fishes
because of its predatory instinct. But by
offering the aquarium foods particular to this
family its appetite will soon be satisfied.

Balistoides conspiculum (Bloch)

Photo : Heather Angel

Odonus niger (Günther)

Popular name: **Royal Blue Triggerfish, Redfang Triggerfish** or **Black Triggerfish**
Size: 18in (450mm)
Distribution: Tropical Indo-Pacific

This is probably the most common member of this family. Small specimens are quite cheap and are ideal for the more ambitious beginner. They are very undemanding in their food requirements and will take almost any form of fresh protein, such as clam or mussel flesh, shrimp or small strips of fish. Even flake or freeze-dried foods will be taken.

In *O. niger* the posterior dorsal, anal and caudal fins are much longer than those of other Triggerfishes and tend to give a flowing effect when the fish is swimming.

Rhinecanthus aculeatus (Linnaeus)

Popular name: **Hawaiian Triggerfish** or **Humu-humu-nuku-nuku-a-puaa** (Hawaiian)
Size: 10in (250mm)
Distribution: Tropical Indo-Pacific and West Africa

Care should be taken when handling this species if the aquarist values his fingers! Feeding does not present much of a problem, although fresh protein is normally preferred. Algae are eaten, along with flake and freeze-dried food occasionally, but as with most coral fishes there is no substitute for the real thing. This fish bears an unusual marking around the head, comprised of horizontal lines extending from the corners of the mouth, giving an exaggerated impression of the overall size of the mouth.

Young specimens are well suited for a community tank, but the older and larger ones should never be kept with small fishes.

Rhinecanthus rectangulus (Bloch & Schneider)

Popular name: **Belted Triggerfish**
Size: 9in (230mm)
Distribution: Hawaii, Indo-Pacific, Red Sea

Somewhat similar in appearance to *R. aculeatus* until one looks closely, *R. rectangulus*, is not so frequently seen in the shops, although it is relatively common in its natural habitat. Like most members of this family it has a marked aggressive tendency. Once it has been well established in an aquarium, though, it will thrive and become quite a character! Personal experience with this species has indicated that occasional specimens travel badly. This may be due to the adverse effects of being drugged prior to transportation, or possibly a weaker strain from certain areas of the ocean; this yet remains unproved.

Blenniidae (Blennies)

Including the following genera:

Aspidontus	Ophioblennius
Blennius	Pholidichthys
Cirripectes	Runula
Ecsenius	Stanulus
Istiblennius	

Widespread in both warm and cold seas, these little fishes can easily be identified by their long dorsal fins.

Often they are attractively coloured and make good aquarium inhabitants, providing the tank is well furnished with rocks and corals for them to hide in.

Blennies are quite intelligent and may even be taught to feed from the hand. In the wild they will often climb out of the water and across the rocks in search of food. They are predators by nature, having very powerful teeth, and are typical bottom feeders.

Some species have no pelvic fins, whilst others have them positioned well forward of the body near the throat. All Blenniidae are scaleless.

This is a charming family of fishes and a great deal of enjoyment can be derived from observing them closely in an aquarium. The more colourful of the Blennies come from the topical seas of the world, the ones from the sub-tropical regions being usually quite drab in colouration.

Most species are peaceful but there are exceptions, such as *Aspidontus taeniatus.*

Popular name: **Peacock Blenny**
Size: 5in (130mm)
Distribution: Mediterranean, East Atlantic

A resilient species which is quite happy when kept at higher temperatures than it would experience in its natural habitat.

Its colouration consists of a liberal sprinkling of peacock-blue spangles on a background of pale fawn to deep charcoal-grey.

Food for this fish should include scraps of shellfish that it can pick up, at will, off the tank floor. It is a bottom-dwelling fish and prefers to spend part of the time hiding among the rocks and corals. It is a species which can be bred in an aquarium and I would recommend it for the beginner.

Blennius pavo (Risso)

Popular name: **Convict Blenny**
Size: 6in minimum (150mm)
Distribution: Indo-Pacific

Juvenile specimens are black with a longitudinal stripe, which may vary from pale gold to silver, and a silver belly. In adult specimens the stripe disappears to be replaced by a dozen or so vertical bands, silver to gold in colouration, and the body is much stockier and darker.

In the US the Convict Blenny is sometimes erroneously called 'Neon Goby'. Feedings of frozen or live brine shrimp or tubifex will be accepted. Plenty of coral and rock cover should be provided under which it can excavate a hollow and set up home.

Pholidichthys leucotaenia   Photo: Richard Ashby

Parrotfishes have large teeth fused together to form a kind of beak. With this beak they bite off chunks of coral and chew them. They obtain nourishment from the algae and minute coral polyps and excrete the coral rock as sand. Over a period of time shoals of these fish can convert tons of coral into sand.

Fishes of this family are to be found in all tropical seas and are usually attractive and very brightly coloured. They have large scales and, because of their beak-like mouth, they should be handled with great care. At night these fish usually wedge themselves into a crevice or some other appropriate resting place until the morning. Some even build a mucous cocoon around themselves at night as an extra protection against predators that rely on their olfactory senses for obtaining food.

Callyodontidae (Parrotfishes)

Including the following genera:

Bolbometopon	Leptoscarus
Callyodon	Scarus
Cryptotomas	Sparisoma

Bolbometopon bicolor (Ruppell)

Popular name: **Two-colored Parrotfish**
Size: 18in (460mm)
Distribution: Indo-Pacific, Red Sea

Young Two-colored Parrotfish are distinguished from others of this genus by the black-edged orange band around the head and the dark ocellus on the dorsal fin. In a mature fish this spot is missing and the once-white body becomes darkened ventrally. This drastic type of colour change is common to many coral fishes and has frequently caused confusion amongst professional and amateur taxonomists.

In an aquarium this fish will, after a period of settling in, accept brine shrimp in any form and live tubifex worms.

Scarus taeniopterus (Desmarest)   Photo: Bruce Coleman

Popular name: **Striped Parrotfish** or **Princess Parrotfish**
Size: 11in (280mm)
Distribution: West Indies and Bermuda

One of the most outstanding features of the Parrotfish family are the markings on the dorsal and anal fins; these are usually highly coloured and play an important part in the overall body colouration. Male fish exhibit more brightly coloured markings than the females, which are generally drab in comparison. This is particularly evident in this species.

Once installed in a largish aquarium, it will flourish on a diet of adult brine shrimp or chopped prawns supplemented with tubifex; often freeze-dried or flake food will be taken, depending on the individual fish.

Male Striped Parrotfish (*Scarus taeniopterus*)
Photo: Bruce Coleman

'Defensive fishes' would be a good descriptive name for these three families which all have highly effective defence mechanisms. As the colloquial name implies, the Pufferfishes blow themselves up into large balls to ward off any would-be attacker. The Porcupinefish also inflates itself to form a spiny ball, although once inflated the water is hard to get rid of and, after an attack, the unfortunate fish usually finishes up bobbing about helpless and at the mercy of the currents.

Blowfishes also swallow water to inflate themselves, and as an extra deterrent their flesh is usually poisonous. *Canthigasteridae* (Sharp-nosed Puffers) *Diodontidae* (Porcupinefishes) and *Tetraodontidae* (Blowfishes) all have a complete absence of ventral fins.

The Pufferfishes are usually brightly coloured and found in warm parts of the Indo-Pacific. The Porcupine and Blowfishes are normally more sombre in colouration.

The food requirements of all these fishes are wide and varied, and it is better to give them plenty of space in a well-aerated tank.

Canthigasteridae, Diodontidae and Tetraodontidae
(Pufferfishes, Porcupinefishes and Blowfishes)

Including the following genera:

Arothron	Diodon
Canthigaster	Sphaeroides
Chilomycterus	Tetraodon

Arothron nigropunctatus (Schneider) Photo: Bruce Coleman

Popular name: **Yellow- or Black-spotted Puffer**
Size: 10in (250mm)
Distribution: Indo-Pacific as far as Polynesia

This species is quite rare in the aquarium world. The body colour is dull yellow with an irregular pattern of black spots. In adult fish the normally parchment-like skin develops short spines.

Feedings of shrimp, mussel or squid will usually keep it in prime condition. Though normally placid by nature, I would not advocate it as a beginner's fish due to the difficulty often encountered in feeding newly introduced specimens.

I know of one large and very beautiful adult fish in a private aquarium in West Germany that is so tame it will poke its head out of the water at feeding time as if in expectation of its daily ration of food.

Canthigaster bennetti (Bleeker)

Popular name: **Sharp Nose Puffer** or **Bennett's Sharp Nose Puffer**
Size: 4in (100mm)
Distribution: Tropical Indo-Pacific

This pleasant species is found in relative abundance throughout the Indo-Pacific. In an aquarium it proves to be quite hardy, accepting readily the tank conditions and the food offered. It is a peaceful fish like all the other members of this particular genus and would make an ideal addition to any community set-up. In their natural habitat, the Sharp Nose Puffers have a varied diet, but are also able to bite off the tips of coral growths with their razor-sharp teeth in order to obtain food. This is a feeding habit normally associated with the Parrotfishes.

Popular name: **Sharp-nosed Puffer**
Size: 5in (130mm)
Distribution: Red Sea, Indo-Pacific, Hawaiian
Islands

This fish is often referred to as *C. marginatus*;
however the correct scientific name is *C.
solandri*. Specimens are easily obtainable and
they are very hardy once acclimatised to
aquarium conditions.
A diet of frozen or freeze-dried brine shrimp
will satisfy its feeding requirements.
The fins are clear with the exception of the
caudal fin, which carries similar markings to
that of the rest of the body and is normally
held closed, but when opened proves to be
quite large in relationship to the rest of its
body. The mouth is well adapted for scraping
minute edible forms of life from the tips of
coral heads.

Canthigaster solandri (Seale)

Popular name: **Sharp-nosed Puffer**
Size: 2in (50mm)
Distribution: Tropical and Indo-Pacific

This, and other members of this genus, will
emit grunting noises if provoked or upset, and
this phenomenon is particularly apparent if
they are netted out of the water for some
reason or other.
The size given above is probably an under-
estimation, but it is at this size that this species
is most colourful and suitable for a marine
aquarium.
Relatively scarce, it is a good community fish
providing the fishes it is living with are not
too large or troublesome.

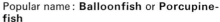

Canthigaster valentini (Bleeker)   Photo: Bruce Coleman

Popular name: **Balloonfish** or **Porcupine-
fish**
Size: 34in (850mm)
Distribution: Circumtropical

There are several species of *Diodon*, but this
species is by far the most common.
The Porcupinefish, as it is generally known,
gets its name from the fact that it has a
covering of short spines. Normally these
spines lie almost flat against the body, but
when disturbed or frightened it will inflate
itself and erect its many spines; the fish then
becomes virtually a ball of spikes and this
formidable object bobbing in the water is
usually enough to deter even the most
persistent predator.
It does well in an aquarium and will live quite
happily on a diet of fresh protein, such as
mussel or shrimp flesh, but flake or freeze-
dried foods may be used to supplement this.

Diodon hystrix (Linnaeus)

Sphaeroides spengleri (Bloch)

Popular name: **Bandtail Puffer**
Size: 8in (200mm)
Distribution: Western Atlantic, from
Massachusetts to Brazil, also recorded from
the Eastern Atlantic

The Bandtail Puffer may occasionally be seen
in brackish water, although it is really a true
salt-water fish. It is widespread on both sides
of the Atlantic.
In their wild state they will inflate themselves
whenever danger threatens. In an aquarium
they will also do this, so care must be taken
when handling this species. Sometimes they
have difficulty in deflating themselves, though
this is the exception rather than the rule.
Their diet is varied and all aquarium foods may
be offered. In the sea they subsist on small
shellfish, starfish, marine worms and algae.

Tetraodon fluviatilis (Hamilton)

Popular name: **Freshwater Pufferfish**
Size: 9in (230mm)
Distribution: From India to the Philippines

This is essentially a brackish-water species and
is more often than not sold as a freshwater
tropical fish. Nevertheless it does appear in the
shops fully acclimatised to salt-water like the
specimen here.
It is a very hardy fish and will live on a variety
of fresh and dried foods. A large tank should
be provided for adults because of their size
and, as with all members of this family, they
will inflate themselves to an even larger size if
they are mis-handled or frightened. This fish
is, however, ideal for the beginner.

Chaetodontidae
(Butterflyfishes and Angelfishes)

Including the following genera:

Apolemichthys	Heniochus
Centropyge	Holacanthus
Chaetodon	Megaprotodon
Chaetodontoplus	Parachaetodon
Chelmon	Pomacanthus
Euxiphipops	Prognathodes
Forcipiger	Pygoplites

Coming from most tropical seas, Butterflyfishes are reef dwellers with laterally compressed bodies. They have small mouths and are never happier than when browsing over algae and picking tiny creatures out of coral growths. Because of this some species have an elongated snout to enable the fish to reach far into the coral to obtain food.

Their colouration is usually bright and quite often forms amazingly intricate patterns. They settle down quite well in aquaria but must be provided with a place to hide at night.

Whilst Butterflyfishes are attractive, Angelfishes are truly beautiful. Again, these are to be found in most warm seas but a large percentage come from the Indo-Pacific.

Generally, they grow larger than the Butterflyfishes (the exception being members of the genus *Centropyge*). They are quite territorial: two fish of the same species will fight if kept together, particularly if they are roughly the same size—they have a sharp spine on each operculum which is well suited for this purpose.

Some Angelfishes change colour as they grow; adults may have a quite different colour pattern from juveniles.

Popular name: **Pygmy Angelfish** or **Cherubfish**
Size: 2¼in (60mm)
Distribution: Tropical Western Atlantic

This particular species is one of the more hardy members of this genus. It is quite a shy fish and therefore its aquarium should be provided with plenty of hiding places. Generally it should be given three or four days to settle into its new home, after which most frozen or fresh shellfish will be accepted readily. Frozen shellfish come in a variety of forms, such as razor meat, chopped mussel, squid, shrimp flesh, cockles, bloodworms, tubifex, crab meat, prawn pieces, or a mixture of various shellfish. These are normally available from any reputable dealer. (It is a good idea to keep a selection of these in the freezer so that the food can be varied from day to day.)

Centropyge argi (Woods & Kanazawa)   Photo: Bruce Coleman

Popular name: **Bicolor Cherub, Oriole Angel, Two-coloured Angelfish** or **Vaqueta de dos Colores**
Size: 4in (100mm)
Distribution: Tropical Pacific

This fish is less hardy than *C. argi* but is in great demand among marine aquarists.
It is similar in appearance to *Holacanthus tricolor,* though it does not grow so large. Many members of the genus *Centropyge* are quite territorial. However this trait is not so apparent with this species.
Any difficulty with feeding can be overcome if the aquarist uses live brine shrimp initially, gradually weaning the fish on to frozen shrimp, which is much more convenient, and then experimenting with various prepared foods once feeding in earnest has begun.

Centropyge bicolor (Bloch)

Centropyge bispinosus (Günther)

Popular name: **Coral Beauty** or **Dusky Angelfish**
Size: 6in (150mm)
Distribution: Tropical Indo-Pacific

This is my own personal favourite among the pygmy angelfishes. Often sold as *C. kennedy,* which is not its correct name, it is an extremely attractive creature and unmistakable in appearance.

In an aquarium it does well providing it is given optimum water conditions. Initially it is fussy about the food offered but will soon settle in, after which almost anything will be taken.

It will not tolerate one of its own kind in the same aquarium and usually the two will fight until the weakest succumbs.

A large tank should be provided with plenty of hiding places into which the fish can retire.

It is a good community fish, but definitely not recommended for the beginner.

Centropyge eibeli (Klausewitz)

Popular name: **Tiger Angelfish**
Size: 4½in (115mm)
Distribution: Andaman Sea to East Indies

This is a beautiful pygmy angelfish but difficult to obtain. The basic body colour, as can be seen from the photograph, is reddish-gold. The sides are adorned with thin wavy bars of bright orange and, like the Pearl-scaled Angelfish (*C. vroliki*), the eyes are rimmed with orange.

In an aquarium they should be fed on frozen shell-meat to keep them in peak condition. They are relatively slow growing and are ideal for a community tank.

Centropyge ferrugatus (Randall & Burgess)

Popular name: **Rusty Angelfish**
Size: 4in (100mm)
Distribution: Western Pacific

Ideal for a community set-up, this species is very mild-mannered and will not become a problem at a later date. It even has the ability to handle the aggression of its more boisterous tankmates.

There should be little problem over its diet and specimens will generally feed the day after introduction. All the same, it is not for the beginner, since it will not tolerate adverse water conditions. It should be transferred to another tank at the first showing of any noticeable nitrite level.

67

Popular name: **Lemonpeel Angel** or **Lemonpeel**
Size: 4½in (115mm)
Distribution: Central Pacific

A mild-mannered fish which will only occasionally scrap with its own kind.
It is not a beginner's fish and some experience is required to keep this species successfully.
The Lemonpeel requires regular feedings of freeze-dried or frozen tubifex worms of fairy shrimp. Live brine shrimp may be used as a starting food for the more difficult specimens.
Water conditions: a pH of 8·3 with a zero nitrite reading and a water temperature of 80°F (26·5°C) is ideal.

Centropyge flavissimus (Cuvier)

Popular name: **Pearl-scaled Angelfish**
Size: 5½in (140mm)
Distribution: Widespread throughout the Tropical Indo-Pacific

This fish, with its bright orange-rimmed eyes, is an attractive addition to any community tank. Although it is not brightly coloured, its pearly sides and dark flanks have made it a popular aquarium fish.
It soon makes itself at home and is often aggressive towards other fishes. Most foods are accepted, and this makes it an ideal fish for anyone but the complete beginner.
Most members of this genus are suitable for a community set-up and are among the most attractive of all marine fishes.

Centropyge vrolikii (Bleeker)

Popular name: **Threadfin, Diagonal Butterflyfish** or **Threadfin Butterflyfish**
Size: 8in (200mm)
Distribution: Tropical East Africa and Red Sea to Central Pacific (including Hawaii)

The name 'Threadfin' refers to the elongated rear part of the dorsal fin which the adult of this species develops.
The snout, although slightly more elongated than that of other Butterflyfishes, does not make this fish any more pedantic about the food it eats. Quite the opposite, in fact, it is one of the easier Butterflyfishes to cater for.
It is fairly hardy and makes a good addition to any marine set-up. Because of its wide distribution and usually large numbers, it is relatively low priced. It is very popular and will get along with most fishes of a similar temperament and, providing the water is in good condition, will live long giving excellent value for money.

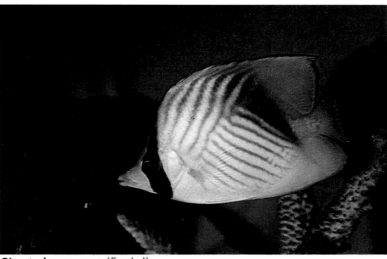

Chaetodon aurega (Forskal)

**Popular name: Mock Eye or Four-eyed
Butterflyfish**
Size: 6in (150mm)
Distribution: Western Atlantic

The white-edged black spot, just forward and
above the caudal peduncle, is called an 'eye
spot'. In its natural habitat this mock eye is
designed to confuse any would-be attacker.
The real eye is disguised somewhat by a dark
line running through it.
In an aquarium it is peaceful and does well on
a diet of frozen and flake foods. Being widespread, it is often seen in the shops at a
reasonable price. It is quite hardy once settled
in an aquarium and feeding well.

Chaetodon capistratus (Linnaeus)   Photo: Bruce Coleman

**Popular name: Orange Butterflyfish or
Pearlscale Butterfly**
Size: 6in (150mm)
Distribution: Indian Ocean

By no means a beginner's fish, in fact it is
quite a shy species. This is a pity because,
although some members of this family lack
bright colours, this fish is truly outstanding.
The peculiar criss-cross markings on its back
are formed by each scale lamina being edged
with black. There is a broad orange band,
edged in white and then in black, which runs
almost the full height of the body and fins
near the tail. The tail itself has an orange stripe
almost at the tip. It is this orange colour that
makes the fish a most attractive addition to an
aquarium, providing the initial timidity and
refusal to eat has passed. This shyness may be
overcome by the thoughtful use of subdued
lighting.

Chaetodon chrysurus (Desjardins)

Popular name: Speckled Butterflyfish
Size: 4in (100mm)
Distribution: Indian and Pacific Oceans

This species is rarely obtainable, despite its
abundance in the Indo-Pacific.
Food is no problem with the Speckled Butterflyfish, and all normal aquarium foods are
suitable. It is quite hardy and relatively easy
to keep.
As with almost all members of this genus, a
black bar runs from the tip of the head down
each side and through the eyes.
It is a small fish but, nevertheless, one worth
keeping if the opportunity presents itself.

Chaetodon citrinellus (Cuvier)

69

Popular name: **Pakistani Butterflyfish** or **Brown Butterflyfish**
Size: 6in (150mm)
Distribution: India, Pakistan, Ceylon to East Indies

Because of past reports about the difficulties involved in keeping this fish, I was slightly concerned when I was given two specimens by an importer friend of mine. They were placed in a well matured 30-gallon (136-litre) tank containing several other species of Butterflyfishes. After ten days of fasting both accepted small pieces of fresh mussel and thereafter never stopped feeding. In the 12 months I had them one specimen (the larger of the two) grew from 3–4in, whilst the 2in specimen hardly grew at all, though its body did become discoid in shape.
Chaetodon collaris may not be a beginner's fish, but I see no reason why the aquarist with a few months' experience of other Butterflyfishes should not attempt to keep this species.

Chaetodon collaris (Günther)

Popular name: **Saddle-back Butterflyfish** or **Black-blotched Butterflyfish**
Size: 8in (200mm)
Distribution: Tropical Pacific

Small specimens of this fish can be purchased quite cheaply and generally do quite well in an aquarium. They grow quite large for a Butterflyfish and should therefore be housed in a suitable tank to allow for this.
Chaetodon ephippium likes a wide variety of foods, including fresh-chopped shrimp and mussel, freeze-dried foods, and flakes. It has a passive nature and is an excellent character fish for a community tank, being well able to take care of itself even against the more boisterous fishes.
Identification is simple due to the presence of a large dark 'saddle' across the rear portion of the back. The underneath of this 'saddle' is edged with a broad white semi-circular band.

Chaetodon ephippium (Cuvier)   Photo: Bruce Coleman

Popular name: **Black-wedge Butterflyfish** or **Saddled Butterflyfish**
Size: 4in (100mm)
Distribution: Central and Indo-Pacific

Although quite shy, it is very hardy indeed and can hold its own with most of the more boisterous species. It is a good community fish but keeps very much to itself.
Variation in S.G., temperature and nitrite content of its environment does not appear to have any marked adverse effect on this fish.
It has 12 dorsal spines which are readily erected when the occasion demands it.
At feeding time this species is not usually the first at the 'table', but if supplied with plenty of fresh or frozen protein it will be one of the last to leave.
Sometimes it can be difficult to get it started on aquarium feeding, especially if it is an adult fish. This, however, can easily be overcome if it is offered frozen adult brine or fairy shrimp.

Chaetodon falcula (Bloch)

70

Chaetodon fasciatus (Forskal)   Photo: Bruce Coleman

Popular name: **Diagonal-lined Butterflyfish**
Size: 6½in (165mm)
Distribution: Indian Ocean, Red Sea

Very similar in appearance to *Chaetodon lunula,* but it can easily be distinguished by the lack of a dark spot on each side of the caudal peduncle.
Both this species and its close cousin can be kept relatively easily in an aquarium as, in my opinion, they are the hardiest of all the Butterflyfishes.
Chaetodon fasciatus can be fed on flake or freeze-dried foods, although, as with most marine fishes, a marked preference is shown for such fresh foods as brine shrimp, mussel or chopped clam.
Generally, it is a peace-loving fish that can grow quite large, so if the fish is to be kept in prime condition adequate space should be provided.

Chaetodon fremblii (Bennett)

Popular name: **Blue-striped Butterflyfish**
Size: 4½in (115mm)
Distribution: Hawaii

This charming Butterflyfish is common only in Hawaiian waters but, because of its numbers, is very often seen in European dealers' tanks. This species is one of the few members of this genus that does not have a dark bar running through the eye. It does, however, have a black spot in front of the dorsal fin.
Although this fish is usually shy at first, it will soon overcome its reticence and will thrive on a diet of freeze-dried or flake food supplemented with regular feedings of fresh protein food forms.

Chaetodon klieni (Bloch)

Popular name: **Sunburst Butterflyfish**
Size: 4½in (115mm)
Distribution: Indo-Pacific

The Sunburst Butterflyfish, although rather mundane in colouration, is a firm favourite with British marine aquarists. It is a delicate looking fish but extremely hardy. Specimens of around 1½–2in (4–5cm) are normally available in the shops, and these are ideal for a community set-up.
After its initial shyness has been overcome, this fish will flourish. It will readily accept most forms of food once it has acclimatised itself to aquarium life. One of the easiest of all the Butterflyfishes to keep.

Popular name: **Blue Chevron Butterflyfish**
or **Red Sea Butterflyfish**
Size: 4in (100mm)
Distribution: Red Sea

The chevron pattern on the sides of this fish
make it easy to distinguish from others. The
striking colouration makes it one of nature's
'gems'. *Chaetodon larvatus* comes only from
the Red Sea and is one of the more difficult
species to keep healthy in an aquarium for any
length of time because of its inability to derive
sufficient nutrients from the usual foods. This
may be overcome by placing it in a well
matured tank containing living coral and
invertebrates on which it can feed. This is an
expensive process unless the aquarist has
access to an unlimited supply of food in this
form. However, specimens will be found that
will accept brine shrimp or some other more
convenient form of food, but this is the
exception rather than the rule.

Chaetodon larvatus (Cuvier)   Photo: Heather Angel

Popular name: **Lined Butterflyfish**
Size: 12in (300mm)
Distribution: Tropical Indo-Pacific

This is another readily available species of
Butterflyfish which has a predominance of
yellow in its colouration. In this case it is one
of several similarly marked species which
occasionally cause taxonomic confusion.
Butterflyfishes, in general, should not be kept
in an invertebrate tank because of their liking
for coral growths. They should, however, be
given a diet which includes plenty of shell-
meat. Live shrimp is also appreciated, though
this is not always available.

Chaetodon lineolatus (Cuvier)

Popular name: **Moon Butterflyfish** or
Red-striped Butterflyfish
Size: 8in (200mm)
Distribution: Indo-Pacific

Like *Chaetodon fasciatus*, aquarium conditions
are not so critical for this species and feeding
presents little difficulty. Most foods are
accepted, including flake or freeze-dried
varieties.
Pattern and colour changes occur during the
life of this fish, particularly around the head.
It is as peaceful as an adult as it is when
juvenile and so is ideal for a community set-up.
In its natural habitat, which is widespread, it
is common and this gives rise to its relative
cheapness. It is also a shallow water fish and
consequently easy for divers to catch.
Specimens are often seen in dealers' tanks and
soon overcome their initial shyness, providing
hours of entertainment for their owners.

Chaetodon lunula (Lacépède)

Chaetodon melanotus (Schneider)

Popular name: **Black-backed Butterflyfish**
Size: 7in (180mm)
Distribution: Tropical Indo-Pacific

The Black-backed Butterflyfish does not respond at all well to the use of drugs for collecting specimens and will usually succumb after a few weeks of captivity. Like many other fishes of this nature, it is not until the fish gets to the hobbyist that the problems over the use of such drugs as sodium cyanide become apparent. I feel that the use of all drugs for collecting aquarium fish should be discontinued, even if this means that the aquarist may subsequently pay a higher price for his specimens.

Furthermore, it would be a good idea for all importers to boycott collectors who use cyanide, dynamite or any other substance that has a physio-chemical or other equally harmful effect on the fishes.

Chaetodon miliaris (Quoy & Gaimard)   Photo: Dr John E. Randall

Popular name: **Lemon Butterflyfish**
Size: 6½in (165mm)
Distribution: Hawaii

This is another Butterflyfish which can be kept with relative ease. It should, however, be housed in a large tank.

The photograph shows an adult specimen of 5½in (140mm) which, incidently, came from Kaneohe Bay, Oahu. It is common only to the Hawaiian Islands and is a charming fellow, lemon in colour, with several dark bars made up of individual black spots running vertically down its sides.

It is a peace-loving community fish and can be fed on most aquarium foods, though its favourite would appear to be fresh mussel. This can best be provided by splitting the mussel in half and serving it on the shell. The empty shells may be removed later and, since this is a natural food, it is often useful for more difficult specimens.

Chaetodon pictus (Forskal)

Popular name: as Latin name
Size: 4in (100mm)
Distribution: Indian Ocean

Often confused with *Chaetodon vagabundis*, this fish has much darker flanks, and the caudal markings differ somewhat.

Chaetodon pictus is often imported with gill flukes (*Monogenea*), and unless suitably treated the fish will soon succumb. Purchasing specimens that continually twitch or flick themselves off prominent objects should be avoided at all costs.

It is a friendly fish that will quickly learn to take dried foods, even from its owner's fingers. It is peaceful and makes an ideal community fish, but will not tolerate a high nitrite level. Whilst it is by no means a beginner's fish, it may be kept by the aquarist with a few months' experience with easier species.

Popular name: Coral Butterflyfish
Size: 5in (130mm)
Distribution: Throughout the Western Pacific

This fish does quite well in captivity and a shoal of seven or eight in a large tank makes an attractive display.
Its natural diet is varied and in an aquarium, once settled, it will accept most foods including the flaked variety.

Chaetodon plebius (Cuvier & Valenciennes)

Popular name: Puerto-Rican or Banded Butterflyfish
Size: 6in (150mm)
Distribution: Western Atlantic

Although this fish is most common in the Caribbean, it is also widespread in most areas of the tropical Atlantic, and even occurs north to Cape Cod in the summer.
On introducing this fish into the aquarium the lights should be turned out to minimise shock, and the new owner should try to avoid any undue disturbance near the aquarium. These precautions will ensure that the fish has the maximum chance of survival.
Feeding can sometimes prove difficult, but providing fresh protein food forms are used this can also be overcome.
Once feeding, *Chaetodon striatus* will prove to be a good community fish, and when housed with other members of this family is an outstanding exhibit.

Chaetodon striatus (Linnaeus)

Popular name: Chevron Butterflyfish
Size: 6in (150mm)
Distribution: Indian and Pacific Oceans, Red Sea

This fish, formerly called *Megaprotodon trifascialis*, is very hard to keep for any length of time, but I feel that it should be included here because of its beauty. It is quite rare occurring singly on the reefs when adult or in small shoals as a juvenile.
In captivity it is strongly territorial and will not tolerate others of the same species. It should be housed in a large tank and fed on living coral if any success is to be hoped for. Some specimens may progress to feeding on live brine shrimp, but this is the exception rather than the rule.

Chaetodon trifascialis (Quoy & Gaimard)   Photo: Bruce Coleman

Chaetodon trifasciatus (Mungo Park)   Photo: Bruce Coleman

Popular name: **Rainbow Butterflyfish** or
Redfin Butterflyfish
Size: 5in (130mm)
Distribution: Indo-Pacific Ocean to Africa

Although imported fairly regularly, this
particular species of Butterflyfish has little
chance of surviving any length of time in an
aquarium. This is unfortunate because it really
is a beautiful fish. Moreover, it generally has a
peaceful temperament and may be kept in a
community set-up. The drawback is, however,
its inability to accept the water conditions in
even the best marine aquaria. An added
problem is finding a diet sufficiently attractive
and nourishing to enable it to survive and
flourish.

I feel that it would be far better to leave this
and other fishes of this nature on the reef
where they may live quite happily and may be
viewed, at will, in their natural habitat.

Photo: Bruce Coleman

Popular name: **Vagabond Butterflyfish**
Size: 5in (130mm)
Distribution: Red Sea, Indo-Pacific

Like *Chaetodon pictus*, which it closely
resembles, this fish is ideal for a community
aquarium. It is peaceful and much more hardy
than its close cousin.

Feeding is seldom a problem, and it will soon
learn to take flake or freeze-dried foods. It
does, however, require a large tank in which
there are plenty of places to hide and browse
around. For sheer delicacy in an aquarium,
there is nothing to surpass the beauty of a
butterflyfish picking and browsing over an
artificially created coral garden.

Chaetodon vagabundis is widespread in its
distribution and is often seen in dealers' tanks.
It is usually cheap and will flourish under ideal
conditions.

above: adult

left: juvenile

Chaetodon vagabundis (Linnaeus)   Photo: Bruce Coleman

Popular name: **Chelmon, Copper-band Butterflyfish** or **Indo-Pacific Longsnout Butterflyfish**
Size: 6½in (165mm)
Distribution: Indo-West Pacific

If a feeding specimen can be obtained it is well worth having. However, if this is not possible then the aquarist would be advised to keep clear of this species until he has had considerable experience of introducing fish to foods that are, in most cases, extraordinary to their diet. That is not to say that this species is impossible to keep in a marine life-support system, but it is by no means easy. Once settled in and feeding, this somewhat delicate fish will readily accept most tidbits. It is rather susceptable to the viral infection *lymphocystis*, and when this disease shows itself it is quite hard to rid the fish of it.

Chelmon rostratus (Linnaeus)

Popular name: **Majestic Angelfish** or **Blue-girdled Angelfish**
Size: 16in (400mm)
Distribution: Philippines, Indo-Pacific

No description could do justice to this beautiful species but, often imported at 2–3in (50–70mm), is a rather difficult fish to keep. Optimum tank conditions are a must for this fish and feeding, although difficult at first, becomes less of a problem as the fish learns to take brine shrimp, tubifex and algae or chopped lettuce.
Acclimatisation is the main problem as it is very timid when newly introduced. It will usually hide behind a rock or piece of coral, sometimes for days on end, seldom venturing out at all let alone feed. However, providing the aquarist is patient, it will usually overcome this reticence.

Euxiphipops nevarchus (Cuvier & Valenciennes)

Popular name: **Six-barred Angelfish**
Size: 20in (510mm)
Distribution: Tropical Indo-Pacific

Whilst not as colourful as others of this genus, this Angelfish is nevertheless striking in its own way.
This is quite a large fish and should therefore be provided with a tank of sufficient size to accommodate it. Set rules cannot be laid down for the feeding of any Angelfish and this species is no exception, but with a little experience the aquarist should be able to overcome the problem.

Euxiphipops sexstriatus (Cuvier & Valenciennes)

Popular name: Blue-faced Angelfish or **Yellow-faced Angelfish**
Size: 18in (460mm)
Distribution: Indo-Pacific

On finding itself in a totally different environment to that which it has been used to, this species will, after a short period of shock, become inquisitive and eventually hungry. If all the precautionary measures concerning the tank and water have been taken care of, and these *must* be optimum, then correct feeding is the only difficulty.

It will become quite friendly and does well on a diet of brine shrimp, frozen shrimp, tubifex, mussel and green stuff.

Euxiphipops xanthometapon (Bleeker)

Popular name: Long-nosed Butterflyfish
Size: 8½in (215mm)
Distribution: Indian and Pacific Oceans from Africa to Mexico

A very beautiful fish, not unlike a real butterfly. It is bright yellow with a purplish-black forehead. The snout is very long, and in the wild this is used to enable the fish to extricate morsels of food from crevices in the coral upon which it grazes.

The Long-nosed Butterflyfish is quite an addition to a marine set-up, although it is not recommended for the beginner.

Its food requirements are not too unusual, and once it has been induced to feed it will live happily on a diet of dried foods with a twice-weekly supplement of fresh protein.

In captivity they are quite hardy, but consideration should be given to choosing tank-mates of the same temperament, which is mild.

Forcipiger flavissimus (Jordon & McGregor)

Popular name: Bannerfish, Wimple or **Poor Man's Moorish Idol**
Size: 8in (200mm)
Distribution: Tropical Indo-Pacific, Red Sea, Hawaii

Easy to keep, the Bannerfish becomes very tame and can be taught to feed from the hand. Three or four can really enhance the appearance of a community tank.

The body is disc-shaped, silvery and strongly compressed. It is not choosy about its food in captivity and will take dried foods readily.

It is a graceful fish and one of my personal favourites. Plenty of free swimming space should be provided for maximum success with this specimen. The young Bannerfish quite often exhibits the cleaning habit of *Labroides dimidiatus*.

Heniochus acuminatus (Linnaeus)

Popular name: **Brown Wimple Fish** or
Humphead Banner Fish
Size: 8in (200mm)
Distribution: Tropical Pacific, Indo-Australian
Archipelago

This is a recent and welcome new species to
the world of marine fish keeping.
The body shape is almost triangular and
laterally compressed. Adults have a hump-like
protuberance on the forehead, though this is
absent in juveniles.
Heniochus varius is a shy species and,
although it may at first seem unaffected by
being introduced to an aquarium, this is
usually an indication of shock. Every possible
precaution should be taken to avoid
exacerbating this state, and if this species is
given the chance it will recover and
subsequently flourish.
This genus contains may beautiful species.

Heniochus varius (Cuvier)

Popular name: **Blue Angelfish**
Size: 18in (460mm)
Distribution: Tropical West Atlantic

Juveniles of this and the following species are
almost identical in colouration, making it very
difficult to differentiate one from the other.
Adult specimens, however, are more easily
distinguished. Colouration of an adult
specimen differs greatly from its juvenile stage,
but a mature fish can be distinguished from
H. ciliaris by the lack of an edged 'crown' on
its forehead. The gill plate is tipped with blue,
and more yellow appears on the dorsal and
anal fins. *H. isabelita* grows quite large, but is
ideally suited for a large display tank. Care
should be taken when handling the Blue
Angelfish, as it is equipped with sharp spines
which can inflict painful wounds. These are
situated on each side of the head just forward
of the gill opening.

Holacanthus isabelita (Jordan & Rutter)

Popular name: **Queen Angelfish**
Size: 18in (460mm)
Distribution: Tropical West Atlantic

The name Queen Angelfish is derived from the
fact that the adult carries a black patch on its
forehead rather like a crown, this being edged
in blue. The body is deeply compressed with
long flowing dorsal and anal fins which
extend out past the tail.
Since, like the preceding species, this fish
grows to quite a size it should be provided
with plenty of swimming space. The Queen
Angelfish requires plenty of live or fresh-
frozen foods and can also be induced to accept
dried or freeze-dried foods, but these latter
two food forms should not be made the staple
diet.

Holacanthus ciliaris (Linnaeus)

Popular name: **Townsend's Angelfish**
Size: 16in (400mm)
Distribution: Tropical Atlantic

This fish has in the past caused a certain amount of controversy. It is, in fact, a hybrid of *H. isabelita* and *H. ciliaris*. Whilst it is not strictly correct to include it as a separate species I have done so because these hybridised variations often appear in the shops under almost every permutation of scientific names applicable to this genus.

Colouration is between the Blue and Queen Angelfishes, and like these two species there are several colour phases.

H. townsendi is no more or less hardy than its true parents and its feeding and maintenance do not differ either.

Holacanthus townsendi

Popular name: **Rock Beauty**
Size: 24in (610mm)
Distribution: Caribbean

When young this fish is bright orange-yellow with a black spot, edged in blue, adorning each side of the body. The eyes also contain a proportion of blue colouration.

As the fish grows the black spot increases in size until it finally covers two-thirds of the body. Occasionally, in prime specimens, the anal fin is tipped with a glowing red colour.

Feeding is not difficult; this species will accept most of the usual aquarium foods, which should be supplemented with green stuff. If no algae is present then chopped lettuce or spinach should be used as a substitute.

This fish is not particularly suited to a small community tank, as it is inclined to be a bit of a bully; an increase in its tank size will minimise this problem.

Holacanthus tricolor (Bloch)

Popular name: **Flagfin Angelfish** or **Three-spot Angelfish**
Size: 10in (250mm)
Distribution: Tropical Indo-Pacific

Though harder to keep than the last species, this fish is just as colourful. The basic body colour is bright yellow, interrupted by three blue-black spots as the Latin name implies (*tri-maculatus*: three-spotted). One spot is on the forehead and the other two on each side of the head. Identification is made easy by the presence of the broad dark band on the lower edge of the anal fin. The mouth is ringed in blue.

This fish will accept live brine shrimp, but is by nature a 'picky' feeder. It fares better when provided with plenty of cover in which to hide. The tank should be large and well aerated.

Holacanthus trimaculatus (Cuvier & Valenciennes)

Popular name: **Ocellate Butterflyfish**
Size: about 5in (125mm)
Distribution: Tropical Indo-Pacific

The Ocellate Butterflyfish is not one of the highly coloured members of this genus, but it is, however, extremely attractive and very popular with marine aquarists. Hitherto unknown, it has proved ideally suited to a marine aquarium due to its undemanding nature. The wise aquarist will nevertheless supply it daily with adequate fresh or frozen food.

The tank should have a decor including plenty of hiding places for this fish, preferably with a quantity of living rock on which it can browse for morsels of the food that it would find in its natural habitat.

Parachaetodon ocellatus (Bloch)

Popular name: **Blue Ring Angelfish**
Size: 16in (400mm)
Distribution: Tropical Indo-Pacific

Members of the genus *Pomacanthus* undergo probably the most dramatic colour changes of all fish. As juveniles they show a striking pattern of blue and white vertical lines on an even deeper blue background.

However, as can be seen from the photograph, the adult fish bears no resemblance to its young.

As with all Angelfishes, the rule is only one per tank and I have yet to come across two large Angelfish of the same species living together peacefully.

After a period of 'weaning' on fresh mussel or shrimp, etc, the newly introduced Blue Ring Angelfish will develop a taste for freeze-dried and flake food and will do well providing the owner ensures the water is without organic or chemical pollution.

Pomacanthus annularis (Bloch)

Popular name: **Black Angelfish** or **Grey Angelfish**
Size: 18in (460mm)
Distribution: Tropical Atlantic

Often confused with the French Angelfish (*P. paru*), the adult Black Angelfish has a lighter body colour. A striking similarity occurs with juveniles of the two species, but the young *P. paru* can be identified through having less yellow in the tail and a head band that does not completely circle the mouth. As far as aquarium conditions are concerned this fish's requirements are the same as for other members of its family. Juveniles are much more colourful and soon become tame. Feeding a diet of algae and fresh protein such as mysus shrimp and mussel should be adequate for this fish, though an occasional feeding of flake food will be readily accepted.

Pomacanthus arcuatus (Linnaeus)

Pomacanthus imperator (Bloch)

Popular name: **Imperial Angelfish** or **Emperor Angelfish**
Size: 16in (400mm)
Distribution: Indo-Pacific

Whilst the juvenile of this species is somewhat similar in appearance to both the juveniles of *P. annularis* and *P. semicirculatus*, there can be no mistake when one sees it in its adult form. It is truly a magnificent sight. The young Emperor Angelfish has a deep blue background colouration with widely curving blue and white lines which form a complete circle at the tail.

This species can easily be cured of *benedenia*, a disease it is most susceptible to, provided a good medication is used (see Disease Guide), and will feed quite readily on a variety of aquarium foods.

It is not a beginner's fish though, and requires optimum water conditions for a healthy life.

Pomacanthus maculosus (Forskal)

Popular name: **Purple Moon Angelfish** or **Blue Moon Angelfish**
Size: 16in (400mm)
Distribution: Western Indian Ocean, Red Sea

In the Gulf of Suez, where this species is particularly abundant, it is usually found in groups of six or more and make an impressive sight browsing through the coral gardens. Unfortunately, it would require a very large and expensive set-up to be able to duplicate this in the home, and so we must accept second best by keeping only one specimen in an aquarium.

This is probably the easiest Angelfish to keep in captivity and is very undemanding in its food requirements after the initial settling-in period has been overcome. An occasional meal of White Worms (*Enchytrae*) or chopped shrimp will be beneficial.

Pomacanthus paru (Bloch)   Photo: Bruce Coleman

Popular name: **French Angelfish**
Size: 16in (400mm)
Distribution: Tropical West Atlantic

The French Angelfish is inclined to be a little particular about the food it eats, but once it has been conditioned to an aquarium life and diet it will become stronger and stronger. We can only simulate the supply of food that fishes are used to in their natural habitat and it is unfortunate that in quite a lot of cases the aquarist can only supply a poor substitute. The young fish possess bright yellow vertical bands that sweep towards the posterior of the dorsal and anal fins. The basic body colour is black, as can be seen in the photograph (overleaf) of a young adult. A fully grown French Angelfish loses the yellow stripes but retains the yellow within the scale pattern (left).

Popular name: **Koran Angelfish** or **Semicircle Angelfish**
Size: 16in (400mm)
Distribution: Tropical Indo-Pacific

This species also undergoes an acute colour change during the stages from juvenile to adulthood. But in this case it is the young specimens which are much brighter. To distinguish this from other similar young Angelfishes it should be remembered that the blue and white lines form a semicircle on its flanks as opposed to straight lines or circles. The name Koran Angelfish originates from the markings on the tail which are formed during the different phases of colour change. These show some similarity to the ancient Mohammedan inscriptions in the Koran.
This is quite an easy fish to keep and soon learns to accept most foods offered. It is a common Angelfish both in the shops and in the widespread range of its natural habitat.
The photograph above shows a young adult fish in the centre with a juvenile specimen behind. The fish on the right is *Acanthurus lineatus*.

left: a young adult, showing changes in colouration a few weeks later

far left: a young French Angelfish
Photo: Bruce Coleman

Pomacanthus semicirculatus (Cuvier & Valenciennes)

Popular name: **Atlantic Butterflyfish** or **Longsnout Butterflyfish**
Size: 5in (125mm)
Distribution: Tropical West Atlantic

This is one of the few Butterflyfishes found in the Atlantic. It is fairly drab in colour and has a shape typical of this family, the body being strongly compressed. The snout is elongated and the general colour is yellow to yellowish-brown.
Specimens are easily obtainable but, from a personal point of view, there are far more attractive Butterflyfishes available to which I would give preference.
It feeds quite well on a diet of tubifex and bloodworm, with occasional feedings of shell-meat such as scallop or cockle.

Prognathodes aculeatus (Poey)

Popular name : **Regal Angelfish** or **Royal Empress Angelfish**
Size: 9in (230mm)
Distribution : Tropical Indo-Pacific, Red Sea

The young of this fish are easily recognisable by the presence of a dark spot on the soft part of the dorsal fin. At this size, though, they are not often seen and it is specimens of 5in (125mm) or more that one sees in the shops. It should be housed in the largest tank possible and given plenty of cover as it is normally very shy at first. Once the initial shock has passed, though, all the usual Angelfish foods may be used.

Pygoplites diacanthus (Boddaert)

Gobiidae (Gobies)

Including the following genera :

Bathygobius	Gobius
Elactinus	Kelloggella
Eleotrides	Lythrypnus
Gobiodon	Paragobiodon
Gobiosoma	Ptereleotris

The fishes of this family are usually very hardy when kept in captivity, but they have a shy and retiring nature and spend most of their time hiding. They are easy to keep and make good community fish. When not in hiding they can be seen stuck to the glass sides of the tank. This is done by suction discs adapted from their ventral fins which are strong enough to allow the Goby to attach itself to another fish.

In their natural element they are found in tide pools and on the inner side of coral reefs. They are smallish, bottom-dwelling fishes with large heads and no lateral line. Many are brightly coloured and they are found in both warm and cold seas, though specimens from the colder regions have a tendency to be more drab in colouration.

Close study has shown that members of this family have the ability to free other fish of parasites by a sucking action, although this phenomenon is rarely observed, particularly in captivity.

Popular name : **Neon Goby**
Size : 4in (100mm)
Distribution : Tropical Western Atlantic

This fish is not unlike the Cleaner Wrasse (*Labroides dimidiatus*) in colouration, and occasionally performs the same social function. It does, however, appear to prefer larger fish on which it can provide the cleaning service. It is a bottom-dwelling fish that may often be seen perched on some prominent rock or coral head.

In an aquarium it is ideally suited to community life and feeds well on most aquarium foods. A pair of these fish may be induced to spawn, but at the present time no fry have been raised to adulthood. Providing tank conditions and diet are suitable, though, this fish will fare well and live for several years.

Elactinus oceanops (Jordan)

Eleotrides strigatus

Photo: Dr Gerald R. Allen

Popular name: **Golden-headed Sleeper**
Size: 4in (100mm)
Distribution: Tropical Indo-Pacific

Like the genus *Ptereleotris,* this group are closely allied to the gobies. Both genera are burrowers and are often seen hovering above their holes on the reef. This particular species is rarely seen in an aquarium.

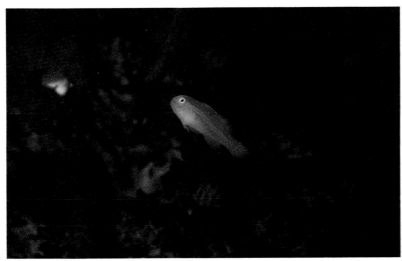

Gobiodon citrinus (Rüppell)

Popular name: **Yellow Goby** or **Goby**
Size: 2in (50mm)
Distribution: Tropical Indo-Pacific

This little fellow is becoming increasingly popular. It is a small fish which seldom exceeds 2in in length and its colour is usually bright yellow.

Several may be kept in the same tank without too many territorial squabbles and, being small it can be kept in a much smaller tank.

As with all members of this genus, the pelvic fins are modified into a sucker-like structure which the goby can employ to hang on to rocks and corals in strong currents. In an aquarium they may be observed hopping from rock to rock, pausing occasionally to search for some morsel of food.

Ptereleotris tricolor (Smith)

Popular name: **Rocket, Arrowfish** or **Scissortail**
Size: 3½in (90mm)
Distribution: Tropical Indo-Pacific

Although not a true goby, this genus is closely related and therefore indicated here. It is a familiar fish in dealers' tanks and, although essentially a burrowing fish, is often seen hovering near the surface as in the photograph.

It is a hardy fish but requires plenty of free swimming space. Most foods are accepted and this makes it ideal for the beginner. It is not an expensive fish and settles down quite well to tank life.

Haemulidae and Plectorhynchidae
(Grunts and Sweetlips)

Including the following genera:

Anisotremus	Haemulon
Diagramma	Plectorhynchus
Gaterin	Spilotichthys

These two families are very closely related and have been combined here, although their habits differ considerably. Members of the family *Plectorhynchidae* can be found in Indo-Australian waters, usually in shoals or groups in the warm shallows. They are 'omnivorous' and adult colouration sometimes varies from that of the young. Nevertheless, their colours are usually very striking. In an aquarium they should be provided with plenty of space and live food for maximum success.

Species from the family *Haemulidae*, however, are widely distributed in the West Indies and off the Atlantic seaboard of the United States. They are relatively easy to keep and can make the most extraordinary noises by grinding their pharyngeal teeth (throat teeth) together. The sound of this is amplified by the swim bladder which acts as a resonator.

Popular name: **Lined Sweetlips or Striped Sweetlips**
Size: 18in (460mm)
Distribution: Indian and Pacific Oceans

The Striped Sweetlips is common throughout the Indo-Pacific and when small makes an ideal addition to a marine aquarium. As it grows, though, so does the problem of keeping the fish in a tank of sufficient size to house its ultimately large proportions. For this reason adults are seldom seen in captivity, except perhaps in zoos.

In an aquarium they prove to be quite hardy and will feed readily on most fresh or frozen foods such as squid, mussel or whitebait. They cannot be trusted with small tank-mates.

Gaterin liniatus (Linnaeus)

Popular name: **French Grunt**
Size: 11in (280mm)
Distribution: Tropical Western Atlantic

This Grunt makes a novel addition to an aquarium. It gets its name from the peculiar noise it makes by grinding its throat teeth together.

All Grunts are shoaling fish and may often be seen in large numbers on the reefs of the Tropical Western Atlantic.

It is a magnificent sight to see half a dozen of these fish in a large tank of, say, 150 gallons (680 l). Any tank smaller than this is unsuitable, unless only one or two are kept, because they require plenty of free swimming space.

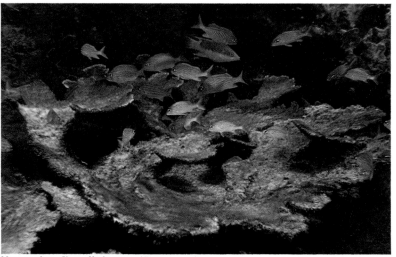

Haemulon flavoliniatum (Desmarest)   Photo: Bruce Coleman

Plectorhynchus albovittatus (Rüppell)

Popular name: **Yellow-lined Sweetlips**
Size: 8in (200mm)
Distribution: Central Indo-Pacific

The Yellow-lined Sweetlips is quite a shy
species in an aquarium but nevertheless it is
very hardy. It does extremely well on a diet of
tinned shrimp and freeze-dried foods.
The ideal tank for this species should include
plenty of crevices and caves in which it can
hide. Imported specimens are generally 3–4in
(75–100mm) long and at this length they are
suitable for an aquarium. They are fairly
colourful, their stripes being a mixture of dark
browns and yellows, and they may
sometimes be confused with the Oriental
Sweetlips (*P. orientalis*).

Plectorhynchus chaetodonoides (Lacépède) Photo: Dr Gerald R. Allen

Popular name: **Clown Sweetlips** or **Polka-dot Grunt**
Size: 16in (400mm)
Distribution: Tropical Indo-West Pacific

When young this Grunt resembles a clown
fish in body shape and mode of swimming.
This is a difficult fish to keep successfully.
Some specimens can be induced to feed quite
heartily, but in the long run it is a matter of
luck whether one gets a feeding specimen or
not.
They grow quite large too, and with growth
the markings alter. They can possibly be
tempted with mysus shrimp, fresh brine shrimp
or fresh mussel, but I have found that the
chances of them taking dried food with relish
is pretty remote.
The young specimens show large white spots
on a dark brown background, but these
become fewer as the fish gets older.

Plectorhynchus orientalis (Bloch)

Popular name: **Oriental Sweetlips**
Size: 6in (150mm)
Distribution: Indian and Pacific Oceans

This is one of the smaller Sweetlips and has
plenty to offer the aquarist. The hardiness of
this fish alone would sell it to most beginners,
but it is when several are housed together that
this species really comes into its own. In this
manner feeding also becomes less of a
problem and they make an attractive display in
small shoals, being always on the move. The
diet should consist of most fresh protein food
forms normally available for marine fishes, all
of which will be taken with apparent relish.
It is often confused with the Yellow-lined
Sweetlips (*P. albovittatus*) which has yellow
stripes, whereas on this species the stripes are
nearly white.

Popular name: **Painted Sweetlips**
Size: 20in (510mm)
Distribution: Tropical Indo-Pacific

As a juvenile this species adapts well to aquarium life. The adult, however, is often too large for the average aquarium and quite unattractive. It has a silvery grey body with a covering of dark spots and flecks.

It is the young fish that one usually sees in the shops, and at this size (2–3in) they are striking and well worth keeping.

Food for this species should be comprised of frozen brine shrimp or mysus, supplemented with freeze-dried foods and green stuff such as algae, or finely chopped spinach.

Spilotichthys pictus (Thunberg)

Holocentridae (Squirrelfishes)

Including the following genera:

Adioryx	Holotrachys
Holocentrum	Myripristes
Holocentrus	Plectrypops
Ostichthys	

Found in shallows around the coral reefs of most tropical seas, Squirrelfishes are nocturnal. They stay hidden in caves during the day, coming out only at night to hunt for small fish, worms and shellfish. They are predators by nature and have big eyes and rather stocky bodies, with scales that are rough to the touch. Colouration is quite bright and nearly always red or red-brown, occasionally with silvery stripes running horizontally along the body to the tail. Adult size is, generally, not particularly large and, in an aquarium, they have a rather shy and retiring nature due to their nocturnal habits. They do well, though, and are quite hardy providing they are given plenty of places to hide. Because of their predatory nature they should not be trusted with small fish, for their nocturnal habits. They do well though and are quite hardy Some species have a long spine that is formed by the extended first ray of the anal fin; in others this is represented by a shorter spike.

Popular name: **Barred Squirrelfish**
Size: 8in (200mm)
Distribution: Indo-Pacific

The Barred Squirrelfish is ideally suited to a home aquarium. It is peaceful when kept with other large fishes and will spend much of its time cruising round the tank.

Most Squirrelfishes are fairly shy, particularly when newly introduced to an aquarium, but my experience of this fish has been that it seldom exhibits this characteristic.

It will accept most frozen food, especially as it falls through the water. If the food goes unnoticed and reaches the bottom then it will probably not be eaten at all. A bottom-feeding fish in the same tank will enable any uneaten food to be taken care of. A good fish for this job would be the Coral Catfish (*Plotosus anguillaris*).

Adioryx diadema (Lacépède)

Adioryx rubra (Forskal)

Popular name: **African Squirrelfish**
Size: 9in (230mm)
Distribution: Tropical Indo-Pacific

The African Squirrelfish is widespread throughout the Indo-Pacific region. It is a predator and nocturnal like most other members of this family.

In an aquarium it prefers live food but will accept substitutes in the form of chopped mussel, squid or crab meat.

The introduction of frozen shell-meat in the shops has made it much easier to keep some of the more difficult species of marine fishes, and is just one example of how much easier this hobby has been made over the last few years.

Adioryx spinifer (Forskal)   Photo: Bruce Coleman

Popular name: **Long-jawed Squirrelfish**
Size: 18in (460mm)
Distribution: Indo-Pacific, Red Sea

This is one of the larger Squirrelfishes and is possibly a little too large for the average home aquarium.

The Long-jawed Squirrelfish has no stripes on its body. The back and sides of the fish are red and the belly is creamy-white. It is not a community fish and will quickly eat any small fish with which it is housed. It is, however, attractive even when fully grown, and so deserves inclusion in this book.

Most forms of fresh protein will be accepted, and it should be provided with plenty of cover in its tank.

Adioryx tiere (Cuvier & Valenciennes)   Photo: Dr John E. Randall

Popular name: **Palau Squirrelfish**
Size: 12in (300mm)
Distribution: Tropical Pacific Ocean

The colour plate shows a young adult fish caught at Eniwetok Atoll. As can be seen, it is predominantly red with the ventral, anal and anterior dorsal fins tipped with white. In certain light conditions horizontal bars may be seen running along the sides of the fish. It is interesting to note here that most nocturnal fishes are red in colour.

In an aquarium it should have tank-mates large enough to avoid being eaten by this predator. Feeding and care is the same as for other members of this family.

Popular name: **Squirrelfish**
Size: 10in (250mm)
Distribution: Tropical Western Atlantic

Throughout the world there are about 80
species of Squirrelfishes, but *H. rufus* is
possibly the most graceful. The caudal fin is
deeply forked, the top part of which is
elongated, as is the posterior dorsal. These
characteristics give it a streamlined appearance
and it is a firm favourite among aquarists.
Though not often seen for sale it makes a
good aquarium fish.
The usual bright red colour, so common with
Squirrelfishes, is not so predominant with this
species, and although it is present its basic
body colour is silver traversed by several
brownish red bars.

Holocentrus rufus (Walbaum)   Photo: Heather Angel

Popular name: **Blackbar Soldierfish**
Size: 9in (230mm)
Distribution: Tropical Atlantic

This fish has big beautiful eyes and is a
nocturnal predator by nature. Most nocturnal
fishes have large eyes in order to make use of
the light which is available at night.
It is one of the most attractive members of
this large family, having a black daub on the
opercle which helps to distinguish it from
other members of the genus.
Care and feeding are the same as for other
Squirrelfishes and Soldierfishes.

Myripristes jacobus (Cuvier & Valenciennes)

This is probably the most widely represented family in both tropical and temperate regions. Their body shapes can vary considerably between species, but the eating habits vary very little. They are always on the move during the day and feed incessantly. Some species have small mouths and others thick lips. The Wrasses' diet consists of everything from small shellfish to algae. When swimming they usually use their pectoral fins to propel themselves, whilst the tail is used as a rudder.

Quite a lot of members of this family build mucous cocoons around themselves at night and literally lie down and go to sleep. Others tunnel into the sand. They are closely related to the Parrotfishes. In an aquarium they are very hardy once they have settled down and are quite fast growing. They soon learn to take dried foods, but some specimens have an aggressive streak when they reach adulthood.

Labridae (Wrasses)

Including the following genera:

Anampses	Labrichthys
Bodianus	Labroides
Cheilinus	Lepidaplois
Cheilio	Lienardella
Coris	Macropharyngodon
Crenilabrus	Novaculichthys
Doratonotus	Pseudocheilinus
Gomphosus	Stethojulus
Halichoeres	Thallasoma
Hemipteronotus	Verriculis
Iniistius	Xyrichthys

Bodianus axillaris (Bennett)

Popular name: **Coral Hogfish**
Size: 8in (200mm)
Distribution: Tropical Indo-Pacific

Juveniles of this fish are somewhat similar in appearance to the young of *Bodianus diana*. Inspection of the snout will, however, determine which is which. In both species the juveniles are black with white spots, but whilst this species has a white snout, *B. diana* has one which is predominantly black.

The adult Coral Hogfish is very beautiful indeed and soon settles down to tank life. The adult male, seen here, is bicoloured mauve and orange-yellow and is quite different from the relatively drab juvenile.

It is an active fish requiring plenty of space and will enjoy a diet of mixed shell-meat.

Bodianus pulchellus (Poey)

Popular name: **Spotfin Hogfish or Cuban Hogfish**
Size: 9in (230mm)
Distribution: West Indies

The colouration of this fish is remarkable and beautiful and it is one of my personal favourites among all the brightly coloured coral fishes.

It does quite well in captivity and will always be the centre of attraction in any community tank. When choosing its tank-mates make sure that they are not small enough to fit in its mouth—they would have little chance of survival for more than a few hours.

Feeding is the same as for other members of this family.

91

Bodianus rufus (Linnaeus)

Popular name: **Spanish Hogfish**
Size: 24in (600mm)
Distribution: West Indies to Florida and Bermuda

The Spanish Hogfish (on left in photograph opposite), when small, exhibits all the cleaning characteristics of the Cleaner Wrasse (L. dimidiatus) by spending a great deal of the day picking ectoparasites from the skin of larger fishes. When adult, however, this trait is rarely seen.

It is a burrowing fish which, when kept in an aquarium with a good depth of base medium, will be observed disappearing into the sand at night only to reappear the following morning. This characteristic has been developed as a defence mechanism and, in the wild, reduces the chances of it being eaten by nocturnal predators while it is resting.

In a tank if proves to be very hardy and will appreciate a diet of frozen shrimp or fresh mussel. It should not be kept with living crustaceans as these will be eaten, since they form part of its natural diet.

Photo: Bruce Coleman

Coris angulata (Lacépède)   Photo: Heather Angel

Coris formosa (Bennett)

Popular name: **Twinspot Wrasse** or **Clown Labrid**
Size: 48in (1.22m)
Distribution: Red Sea, Indo-Pacific

This fish is not really suitable for an aquarium but if the aquarist is lucky enough to obtain a specimen at 3–4in (75–100cm) then his chances of keeping this fish healthy are greatly increased.

It is a colourful Wrasse and is easily identified by the two black blotches on the dorsal fin. In young specimens these are emphasised by large patches of red on the body just below the spots. As the fish matures, though, the red becomes more obscure.

Acclimatisation should be done carefully and feeding should not be attempted for the first 48 hours. After this time the newly introduced fish will be a little happier with its surroundings and may be tempted with live food such as brine shrimp.

Popular name: **African Clown Wrasse**
Size: 15in (380mm)
Distribution: Indian Ocean

Coris formosa was, at one time, thought to be a colour stage of C. gaimard but this is not so. The young are similar and even now confusion may often occur. The adult fish, pictured here, is characterised by an orange cap on its head and a blue streak which runs diagonally from below the foremost part of the dorsal fin to a point under the eye. The back and sides are dark brown and covered with a series of black spots and bars.

At night this is a burrowing fish so a good depth of base-medium should be present in its tank. Feeding is the same as for others of this family.

Popular name: **Red Labrid, Yellow-tailed Wrasse** or **Clown Wrasse**
Size: 16in (400mm)
Distribution: Tropical Indo-Pacific

When young this Wrasse has markings and colouration similar to that of members of the genus *Amphiprion,* hence its common name. As the fish gets older the red deepens on the body and the black becomes more prominent around the white. The body deepens to black until, as the fish reaches maturity, the colouration has changed completely to a rich mauvish body with a red dorsal and anal fin edged in blue. A brilliant blue line appears, running from the top of the head across the opercle and round the underside of the eye to a point just behind the snout. The caudal fin becomes bright yellow. Although shy at first, this species will settle down quite well to aquarium life and feeds well. It should be given plenty of room.

Coris gaimard (Quoy & Gaimard)

Popular name: **Green Wrasse** or **Dwarf Wrasse**
Size: 3in (75mm)
Distribution: Tropical Atlantic

This fish is common in its natural range but seldom seen in an aquarium, which is a pity because it is a very attractive species. The colouration is an overall lime-green.
It is not a fish that travels well but once settled in an aquarium it will soon start to feed. Plenty of cover should be provided amongst which it can hide. Though not normally a shy fish, care should be taken during the initial introduction to an aquarium so that it is not subjected to any unnecessary stress.
Its diet is quite varied and all aquarium foods will usually be accepted.

Doratonotus megalepis (Günther)

Popular name: **Dragon Wrasse**
Size: 5in (130mm)
Distribution: Tropical Indo-Pacific

This particular Wrasse has an unmistakable appearance, a reasonably placid nature and will settle into a community set-up very well presenting no major problems to the fish-keeper. Several may be kept in the same tank where they will live quite happily.
Food for this species should consist mainly of shell-meat, such as mussel or squid, supplemented with an occasional feeding of live shrimp if it is available. The Dragon Wrasse will not tolerate poor water conditions: plenty of aeration and cover should be provided.

Hemipteronotus taeniurus (Lacépède)

Labroides bicolor (Fowler & Bean)

Popular name: **Bicolor Wrasse** or
Bicolored Cleaner Wrasse
Size: 4½in (115mm)
Distribution: Indian Ocean, Western Pacific

Though the juvenile has a different colour pattern from the adult fish, the yellow rear part of the body is retained throughout its life. Young fish have horizontal stripes of yellow, one above and one below the eye, which run from the snout towards the tail. As the fish grows this yellow fades into white. When adult the bands are not present and the entire front part of the body is blue-black.
Feeding is often a problem since, in its natural habitat, much of its diet is derived from picking parasites from other fishes. This diet may be substituted with items such as live brine shrimp and finely chopped shell-meat.

Labroides dimidiatus (Cuvier & Valenciennes)

Popular name: **Cleaner Wrasse** or
Bicolored Cleaner Wrasse
Size: 4in (100mm)
Distribution: Indo-Pacific

Quite a few members of this family exhibit cleaning activities, but this fish is the best known of them all. It will readily display this trait in an aquarium, providing its owner with a chance to see one of nature's wonders in action. This fish is able to perform this cleaning procedure on large predators too and there seems to be an understanding between them that, providing the Wrasse performs this duty correctly, he will come to no harm.
Occasionally, a Cleaner Wrasse will touch upon some tender spot on the body of the fish it is cleaning, whereupon the fish will give an involuntary twitch, but other than this they do not seem to mind having another fish 'peck' at them, sometimes for minutes on end.

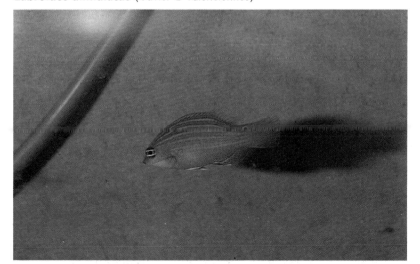

Pseudocheilinus hexataenia (Bleeker)

Popular name: **Pyjama Wrasse** or **Six-lined Wrasse**
Size: 4in (100mm)
Distribution: Tropical Pacific

A very shy and secretive fish which does not attain the large size of many other members of this family. Despite its small size it is extremely attractive and will certainly add something to a community tank. Several may be kept together without territorial squabbles. They may even be kept in an invertebrate tank where two or three specimens, darting in and out of the coral growths, look especially nice.
Feeding, though sometimes a problem, usually becomes 'second nature' in an aquarium.

Popular name: Blue Head
Size: 6in (150mm)
Distribution: Tropical Western Atlantic

A remarkable colour change occurs with the
Blue Head during the transitional stage
between juvenile and adulthood. Once thought
to be a different species, the juvenile has an
overall colour of bright yellow and the tip of
the tail is straight. During the intermediate
stage there are many possible colour variations
until, when adult, the Blue Head earns its
colloquial name.

From the snout to a point just behind the
pectoral fins the head is suffused with blue.
The tail of the adult fish has the top and
bottom rays extending out to give it a
streamlined effect. It is an easy fish to keep
but needs plenty of free swimming space if it
is to be happy. It is an undemanding feeder
and will accept most foods.

Thallasoma bifasciatum (Bloch)

**Popular name: Moon Wrasse, Lunar
Wrasse** or **Lyretail Wrasse**
Size: 12in (300mm)
Distribution: Tropical Indo-Pacific

An aggressive fish which should be housed in
a large tank. It is inclined to grow into a bit of
a bully so care should be taken when
choosing its tank-mates.

It is a magnificent fish, however, and the facial
markings give it a devil-like appearance. It is
relatively easy to keep and will soon settle
down to aquarium life. Fresh protein food
forms are preferred, although freeze-dried and
flake food is also accepted. During the day
this fish is always on the move, propelling
itself around the aquarium using only its
pectoral fins. At night, though, it digs itself
into the sand and will stay there until the
following day. This curious habit has been
developed as a protection against nocturnal
predators.

Thallosoma lunare (Linnaeus)

Popular name: Blue Fin or **Banana Wrasse**
Size: 10in (250mm)
Distribution: Tropical Indo-Pacific

This is one of the most abundant of labrid
fishes in the tropical Pacific (except Hawaii
where it is rare). It also occurs in Japan and
Australia. It is a colourful Wrasse and the male
is characterised by large dark blue areas on
each pectoral fin and several vertical orange
marks on the body. The female pictured here
is a 5in (125mm) specimen caught off the
Marcus Islands.

The juveniles are great favourites with marine
aquarists. Colouration at this stage is bright
yellow, hence the name Banana Wrasse, and
the dorsal and caudal fins show black spots
which may vary in size with age.

It is reasonably easy to keep and it will soon
settle down to a diet of frozen mysus, chopped
mussel and the usual dried foods.

Thallasoma lutescens (Lay & Bennett)   Photo: Dr John E. Randall

Once again these families have been combined due to their close relationship. In this case the sub-family *Pseudochrominae* has been included as well. This sub-family contains the genus *Gramma* and is classified under the *Serranidae*.

Members of the family *Lutjanidae* are to be found singly or in groups in the shallows of most tropical seas. They are quite fast growing and are able to eat a wide variety of foods. However, they are predators and have large mouths equipped with razor-sharp teeth. Their body shape can vary considerably from species to species.

Members of the *Serranidae* also vary in body shape and have large mouths and strong teeth. They do not usually grow quite as large, though, and in an aquarium they should be provided with caves to hide in. They are widespread in both tropical and temperate regions and are usually rather pugnacious. But, in spite of this, they are easy to keep.

Both families accept aquarium life quite happily and soon settle down to tank conditions.

Lutjanidae and Serranidae
(Snappers, Groupers and Sea Basses)

Including the following genera:

Anthias	Lutjanus
Anyperodon	Mirolabrichthys
Cephalopholis	Morone
Chromileptis	Mycteroperca
Dampieria	Pseudochromis
Epinephelus	Roccus
Gramma	Serranellus
Grammistes	Serranus

Anthias squamipinnis (Peters)

Popular name: **Wreckfish, Lyretail Coralfish** or **Butterfly Perch**
Size: 4in (100mm)
Distribution: Tropical Indo-West Pacific

In its natural habitat this fish is found in large shoals. It is one of the most colourful Serranids and ranges from yellow, through orange to pink according to age.

Sexing of this species is made easy since the male is usually more colourful than the female and has an extended third dorsal ray when adult.

It is not for the beginner but can be kept in an aquarium. Feeding this fish may prove difficult at first; often live food is all that a newly introduced specimen will accept. If the aquarist perseveres, chopped mussel or shrimp, introduced at the filter outflow, will appear sufficiently 'alive' to be taken with relish.

Popular name: Pantherfish or **Polka-dot Grouper**
Size: 20in (500mm)
Distribution: Indo-West Pacific

Another species that can be recommended for beginners. The Polka-dot Grouper has a large appetite and an even larger mouth and can take great delight in cutting down the number of fish the aquarist has to feed!
This fish will do well and will soon learn to accept dried foods and other more convenient forms of fresh protein.
It is a furtive fish and will usually adopt a head-down position when resting or lurk about at the back of the tank. At feeding time, or when it chooses to make one of its regular appearances at the front of the tank with widespread fins, it is an impressive sight.
The colouration, together with the enormous fins and small head, give it an air of eccentricity that make a truly interesting species to keep.

Chromileptis altivelis (Cuvier & Valenciennes)

Popular name: Royal Gramma or **Fairy Basslet**
Size: 5in (130mm)
Distribution: Tropical West Atlantic

This beautiful and tiny Grouper is now enjoying more popularity. Several years ago it was hard to keep this fish alive for more than a few weeks, and whilst some people will argue that success now is due to better acclimatisation by the shippers, I prefer to attribute this more to the improvement of the aquarists' fishkeeping techniques and equipment.
In the wild it is found swimming around in caves or crevices or upside-down under ledges. In order to duplicate this the aquarium should be provided with plenty of rocks and corals which can act as cover for it. Its diet should consist of frozen shrimp, clam and similar foods supplemented with occasional feedings of live brine shrimp.

Gramma loreto (Poey)

Popular name: Emperor Snapper, Government Bream or **Red Emperor**
Size: 36in (910mm)
Distribution: Indian and Pacific Oceans

Not a common fish by any means but widespread throughout the Indian and Pacific Oceans. This beautiful species grows fairly large and, because of the amount of food it is prepared to consume, quite quickly too. Large specimens are rare and much sought after.
It is a very handsome fish which, when excited, shows a rosy glow on its flanks. The normal colouration is brownish-black bars on a white background. As the fish matures the bars change to a more reddish-brown.

Lutjanus sebae (Cuvier & Valenciennes)

Mirolabrichthys tuka (Herre)

Photo: Dr Gerald R. Allen

Popular name: **Purple Queen** or **Butterfly Perch**
Size: 5in (130mm)
Distribution: Indo-Pacific

A species which is not often seen for sale but is ideally suited to marine aquarium life. Like its close relative, *Anthias squamipinnis*, this fish does not grow too large. It is exceedingly attractive and easily identified by the proboscis-like extension of the upper lip. In an aquarium it likes a diet of canned shrimp which has previously been washed free of preservative and finely chopped. This food is taken as it falls through the water. Many Serranids, including *M. tuka*, are 'hermaphroditic', meaning that the gonads of both sexes are in one fish. On the reef these fish usually form small schools at depths exceeding 50ft (15m) where they feed on plankton, never straying far from the sheltering coral.

Pseudochromis dilectus

Popular name: as Latin name
Size: 4in (100mm)
Distribution: Indian Ocean around Sri Lanka

This *Pseudochromis* is quite rare, though it is suitable for a marine aquarium. Being extremely attractive, it is usually the centre of attraction in the tank. It is very hardy, having the ability to withstand quite drastic changes in water conditions seemingly with no ill-effects. Normally this fish cannot be coaxed into accepting dried foods in any form; it will take fresh or frozen shell-meat though.
Typical of all members of this genus, the dorsal fin runs for two-thirds of its body length.

Pseudochromis paccagnellae (Axelrod)

Popular name: **False Gramma, Dottyback, Royal Dottyback** or **Paccagnella's Dottyback**
Size: 2in (50mm)
Distribution: Indonesia to Australia

This fish was brought to the attention of ichthyologists primarily by the hobbyists. Its spectacular colours brought it to the attention of collectors. Body colouration consists of chrome-yellow and magenta. Though not shown in the photograph, a narrow white band separates the two colours at the mid-body position. Sometimes this band is only partially present, as on the fish shown. Having kept this fish in an aquarium I know that it is relatively undemanding in its food requirements and will even take flake food. However, it is rather a timid fish and should not be kept with large or boisterous tank-mates. It is, on occasion, erroneously sold as *Gramma loreto*.

Monocanthidae (Filefishes)

Including the following genera:

Acanthaluteres	Navodon
Aluteria	Oxymoncanthus
Cantherines	Pervagor
Ceratacanthus	Stephanolepis
Monocanthus	

These fishes are not unlike Triggerfishes in appearance. In fact their method of swimming is similar. They are masters of disguise and in their natural habitat, when danger threatens, hide head-down among seaweed and thus blend into the background. They also feed head-down on a diet composed mainly of coral polyps. Filefishes can be found in most warm seas, usually among dense vegetation. They have leaf-shaped laterally compressed bodies which are rough to the touch. At one time their skins were used as an abrasive, hence the name Filefish. They have a spiny dorsal fin and a single spine on the belly that can be erected, raising a flap of skin with it.

Because of the nature of these fishes' feeding habits they are not easily kept in captivity, though they can often be persuaded to eat newly hatched brine shrimp, chopped spinach and lettuce. They should be kept in a tank on their own, but if this is not practical then boisterous tank-mates should be avoided.

Popular name: **Tasseled Filefish**
Size: 7in (180mm)
Distribution: Indonesia to Australia

The dorsal and anal fins of this fish, when moved rapidly, provide the necessary propulsion. Even so it is not a fast-moving species and normally relies on camouflage to get it out of trouble in its natural habitat. As is often the case with the Filefishes, it is shy and retiring by nature. It is also a fickle feeder and should be given finely chopped food.

It is easily recognised by the numerous protuberances and wavy markings on its body. Normally this fish may be added quite safely to a community set-up.

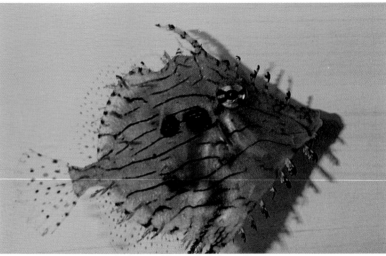

Monocanthus spinosissimus (Quoy & Gaimard)

Popular name: **Orange-green Filefish** or **Longnosed Filefish**
Size: 20in (510mm)
Distribution: Central and West-Pacific

This close relative of the Triggerfish family is peaceful and, once acclimatised, will prove to be an extremely colourful addition to anybody's collection.

Great care must be taken to ensure that adequate cover is provided. In the past I have avoided purchasing specimens with sunken bellies, since some difficulty may be encountered in feeding even prime newly-acquired specimens.

The feeding problem may be overcome with brine shrimp and chopped mussel and an occasional 'treat' of crab flesh.

Oxymoncanthus longirostris (Bloch & Schneider)   Photo: Heather Angel

Pervagor tomentosus (Linnaeus)

Popular name: **Pink-tailed Filefish** or
Red-tail Filefish
Size: 5in (130mm)
Distribution: Indo-Pacific

This is one of the more attractive members of this peculiar family. As the name suggests, this fish has a pinkish-red tail, the remainder of the body varying from silvery-grey to silvery-green.

In an aquarium, feeding can prove to be difficult initially, but this problem can usually be averted to some extent by the use of live foods such as brine shrimp or mysus.

It should not be kept with boisterous tank-mates because of its shy and retiring nature.

Although these two families are not closely related they have been combined here because of their many similarities. Both are brackish water families that inhabit coastal areas and are quite well known to freshwater aquarists, since they can be acclimatised to freshwater. They are good fish for the beginner, being quite hardy and long lasting.

Monos are to be found shoaling around Mangrove roots. They are always on the move and on the lookout for food. Their bodies are laterally compressed and silver in colour, which is particularly attractive if they are kept in shoals in a large aquarium. There is only one genus—*Monodactylus*.

Scats, on the other hand, are found more in estuaries and dock areas around landing piles. They are extremely greedy fish and will eat almost anything. Caring for them presents little or no problem and this makes them very popular.

Members of both these families can be kept in brackish water (a mixture of fresh and salt water). I have found that a specific gravity of 1·015° is ideal, although they can be maintained in water anywhere between 1·000° and 1·028° quite successfully.

Monodactylidae and Scatophagidae (Monos and Scats)

Including the following genera:

Microcanthus	Scatophagus
Monodactylus	Selenotoca

Popular name: **Stripey**
Size: 6in (150mm)
Distribution: Tropical Western Pacific and Hawaiian Islands

The Stripey is particularly abundant in the Hawaiian Islands, Japan, Ryukyu Islands and eastern Australia.

In Hawaii, the young appear in tidepools and shallow water from about December until May, then apparently move to deeper water. These juvenile fish are easily collected with dipnets and are extremely hardy aquarium fish.

In Europe, specimens are a little harder to come by and shipments of these fish are quite rare. This is probably due to their lack of bright colours but, as can be seen from the accompanying photograph, they are still very attractive fish.

Feedings of any aquarium food will suit the Stripey, since it is not hard to please.

Microcanthus strigatus (Cuvier & Valenciennes) Photo: Dr John E. Randall

101

Popular name: Mono or Malayan Angelfish
Size: 5in (130mm)
Distribution: Indian Ocean, Pacific and
Red Sea

This, and the next two species, are primarily
brackish water fishes. The Mono is often seen
in shops and is relatively cheap compared with
true marine fishes. Specimens living in fresh
water can be acclimatised over a period of a
few hours to salt water by carefully adding a
little of the latter at a time. No ill effects are
suffered and, if anything, they appear to fare
better in salt water.

It is a shoaling fish and requires plenty of free
swimming space. The Mono tends to bully
small fish and be bullied by larger fish.

Food is no problem and many particles of food
overlooked or discarded by other fishes are
soon snapped up with relish.

Monodactylus argenteus (Linnaeus)

Popular name: Sea Bat or Moonfish
Size: 6in (150mm)
Distribution: West Africa

The Sea Bat, or Moonfish as it is sometimes
called, can easily be acclimatised to fresh or
salt water. The body pattern and fin formation
is reminiscent of *M. argenteus,* although the
Sea Bat is much deeper bodied.

It grows larger than its close relative and is
less inclined to be bullied by other inhabitants
of a salt water community tank.

It is best kept in shoals of four or more, and is
ever present at feeding time, dashing wildly
about scooping up every morsel of food.
Because of this it is a good teacher of other
fish which may not have learned to feed in an
aquarium.

Monodactylus sebae (Cuvier)   Photo: Heather Angel

Scatophagus argus (Bloch)

Popular name: **Scat** or **Spotted Scat**
Size: 8in (200mm)
Distribution: Indo-Pacific

There are two distinct colour variations of this species. By far the most common is the Black and White Scat. This fish has a silvery body with a liberal covering of black spots, which leave the fins relatively clear of markings. The Tiger Scat, which has large flecks of red around the head and back as well as a generous helping of spots, is much rarer. Scats are normally found in estuaries. Some do find their way onto the reef, but strictly speaking this is a brackish water fish. In a freshwater aquarium this fish has been called an aquarium 'lawnmower' because of the way it devours algae and higher forms of plant life at a tremendous rate. In a sea-water aquarium it should be provided with occasional feedings of chopped spinach or lettuce to keep it in prime condition.

The Moray Eels make up one of the most ferocious families alive in the sea today. They have enormous mouths extending behind their eyes, and very powerful teeth. Often they are unable to shut their mouths completely. Their snake-like shape enables them to lie motionless in a hole and wait for food.

Some of them are brightly coloured and look quite attractive in a fearsome sort of way. All have small gill openings and lack pectoral fins. Their bodies are covered with a thick skin and they have a nostril above each eye.

In captivity, the coral and rocks should be built to form crevices and holes for the fish to hide in and they should be fed on a wide variety of shell-meat.

On the whole, the Morays do not make very good aquarium fish for most are too large or too dangerous, or both, and make problems that the beginner can well do without. For the more experienced marine aquarist they provide an unusual, if not sensational, slant on the fishkeeping hobby.

Muraenidae (Moray Eels)

Including the following genera:

Echidna	Muraena
Gymnothorax	Myrichthys
Lycodontis	Rhinomuraena

Echidna zebra (Shaw & Nodder)

Popular name: **Zebra Moray**
Size: 4ft (1.22m)
Distribution: Red Sea, Tropical Indo-Pacific

The Zebra Moray is a striking and unmistakable fish. It is ideal for the aquarist who has a passion for the bizarre.

In an aquarium it will accept most foods, such as chopped clam, shrimp and mussel flesh. Its tank should be furnished in Moray fashion with plenty of caves and crevices into which it can retire. It is not the most ferocious of its family and is usually seen for sale at a size of 12–18in (300–500mm). Being a large and stocky fish its tank should be large enough to provide ample free swimming space. The fishes with which it is housed should also be sufficiently large if they are not to be eaten by this predator.

Popular name: Blue Ribbon Eel
Size: 40in (1m)
Distribution: Tropical West Pacific

The Blue Ribbon Eel grows too large for the average aquarium and is, in fact, normally sold at a length of about 24in (600mm). This means that it is outside the scope of many aquarists. Even so, it is a colourful addition to the range of fishes available to us.

Provide this fish with plenty of rocks and corals around which it can coil its long ribbon-like body. Care should also be taken to ensure that it is not able to slide out of the tank, which, of course, it will do, with ease, if a tight cover glass is not fitted.

It is a predator and so it should be fed on live fishes or frozen whitebait. Small fishes like the Demoiselles should not be kept in the same aquarium or they will also be eaten.

Rhinomuraena amboinensis (Barbour)

The Trunkfishes are found in most warm seas of the world and feed on small invertebrates, usually where the sea bed is reasonably sandy. They are peculiar fish with hard bony plates underneath their skin. The total absence of ventral fins and their awkward way of swimming makes them even more unusual. Their method of locomotion is by the use of their pectoral, dorsal and anal fins.

In the sea they are not often bothered by predators because of their poisonous skin which, when eaten, can prove deadly to the attacker.

Aquarium specimens are quite shy and feeding can prove something of a problem at first. When one of these fish refuses to feed for any length of time it usually develops concave flanks and subsequently dies. They have small mouths and are rather choosy feeders, but when given the correct diet and optimum conditions they make superb additions to a marine aquarium.

When disturbed or frightened their tail, which is normally straight, folds round and presses flat against the body, rather like a dog with its tail between its legs.

Ostraciidae (Trunkfishes)

Including the following genera:

Acanthostracion	Ostracion
Lactophrys	Tetrosomus
Lactoria	

Popular name: Cowfish or Short-horned Cowfish
Size: 20in (500mm)
Distribution: Pacific and Indian Oceans

No book on coral fishes would be complete without the inclusion of the Cowfish. It remains one of my personal favourites. If fishes have facial expressions then this species has a sad face.

They are easy to keep in an aquarium and, although relatively slow moving, are easy to feed. They may even be bred under tank conditions if the owner is lucky enough to obtain a pair. The eggs are large and free floating; hatching takes place in a little under a week.

The Cowfish is easily recognised by two horn-like appendages on the head. The body is yellow speckled with a myriad of blue spots on the back and sides which decrease in size towards the caudal peduncle.

Lactoria fornasini (Linnaeus)

Popular name: **Spotted Cube**
Size: 8in (200mm)
Distribution: Tropical Indo-Pacific

This Boxfish is, when young, extremely
attractive, being bright yellow in colour
liberally covered with black spots. Its box-like
body and peculiar mode of swimming make it
an ideal choice for a peaceful community
set-up. The adult is a less attractive grey
colour but it still retains the polka-dot pattern.
These fishes should be introduced into an
aquarium with extreme care since any
traumatic shock may cause them to excrete a
highly toxic mucus. In its natural habitat this
is used as a defence mechanism to ward off
would-be predators. However, in the close
confines of a marine tank this mucus will
usually prove fatal to all the tank occupants,
including the poor Boxfish itself.

above: adult

below: juvenile
Photo: Bruce Coleman

Ostracion cubius (Linnaeus)

Platacidae (Batfishes)

Genus: Platax

Although it may not be apparent at first glance, this family is closely related to the Butterflyfishes. However, Batfishes grow much bigger: up to 1in (25mm) per month in captivity! For this reason they need a large tank.

They are usually a leathery brown colour and are widespread throughout the Indo-Pacific region.

Batfishes do not have a shoaling instinct and are normally only found singly or in pairs.

In captivity they are easy to keep and will eat most foods, becoming tame enough to accept tid-bits from their owner's hand. More and more of these fish are now being sold and consequently they are not as expensive as they used to be.

They have quite a personality and can become the main attraction in a tank, in spite of their lack of bright body colour.

Popular name: **Batfish** or **Orbiculate Batfish**
Size: 20in (500mm)
Distribution: Red Sea, Indian and Pacific Oceans

Probably the most common of all the Batfishes, it is an ideal choice for the beginner (provided that he has gained a little experience in keeping Damselfishes and the like) because of its undemanding appetite. Once established it will become a firm favourite with all the family and can live a long time in an aquarium. It will usually be the first there at feeding time and several kept in a large tank make an impressive show.

The body is compressed and disc-shaped and, as with all this genus, the edge of the caudal fin is straight.

Platax orbicularis (Forskal)

Popular name: **Batfish** or **Long-finned Batfish**
Size: 14in (350mm)
Distribution: Indo-Pacific, Red Sea

Platax pinnatus is the least hardy of the Batfishes but it is by far the most beautiful. It is rarely seen for sale and is usually expensive. It is characterised by a scarlet snout and a line which practically encircles its body and fin tips like a halo.

It is similar in shape to *Platax teira*, although the overall colouration is much darker. This species requires fresh protein, but some compromising specimens can be induced to take flake or freeze-dried foods.

The Batfishes, particularly this species and *P. teira*, have a most peculiar defence mechanism: whereas other fishes are armed with poisonous spines or scalpels, these fish shed the mucous coating from their body and fins as they flee from danger.

Platax pinnatus (Linnaeus)

Platax teira (Forskal)

Popular name: **Batfish** or **Long-finned Batfish**
Size: 24in (600mm)
Distribution: Indian and Pacific Oceans and Red Sea

A very fast-growing fish which, if fed on a diet of the usual dried foods and fresh protein, can do well in captivity.
Platax teira is a good-natured fish on the whole, although it is sometimes inclined to bully smaller fish as it gets older.
Feeding presents no problem and flake food is accepted with relish. It becomes hand-tame and, once settled in a tank, will always be seen swimming back and forth at the front. As time goes by this fish will get to know its owner by sight, and can be trained to respond, even to its owner's call.

Marine Catfishes are not unlike their freshwater cousins to keep, although there are some differences. It is not commonly known, but most Plotosid Catfishes roam around algal growths in large shoals, particularly when young. Then, if danger approaches, they quickly mass into a large ball with their tails pointing inwards. As can be imagined, the sight of a large whiskery ball rolling through the water is enough to deter even the most hungry predator.
Their bodies are somewhat elongated and entirely without scales. They have four pairs of barbels around the mouth and utilise these for locating food.
They do well in captivity and can be kept with even the most timid fish when young. However, as they get older they are inclined to get a little more aggressive. Because of their natural shoaling habits it is better if several of the same species are kept together. They are quite fast growing in captivity and possibly rival the Batfishes for growth rate. When netting a specimen, care should be taken to ensure that the fins are not damaged as they sometimes fail to heal up and the fish may then die. The best method is to use a plastic bag instead.

Plotosidae (Catfishes)

Genus: Plotosus

Popular name: **Coral Catfish, Candy-striped Catfish** or **Salt Water Catfish**
Size: 27in (690mm)
Distribution: Tropical Indo-Pacific

This fish seldom reaches over 12in (300mm) in an aquarium despite its insatiable appetite. Having observed this fish closely, I have found that it has very poor eyesight and uses its feelers more than its eyes at feeding time. In captivity it likes to dig tunnels under coral and rocks for a place to hide.
It is quite dangerous, being equipped with venom glands along its dorsal and pectoral spines.
There is a small dendritic organ situated just behind the vent. This pink lobe is composed of cells which are similar to the chloride cells in the gill filaments of fishes and the salt cells of birds. This suggests that the organ functions as a salt excreting gland.

Plotosus anguillaris (Bloch)   Photo: Dr Gerald R. Allen

107

Pomacentridae
(Demoiselles and Clownfishes)

Including the following genera:

Abudefduf	Glyphidodontops
Amphiprion	Microspathadon
Chromis	Neopomacentrus
Dascyllus	Paraglyphidodon
Eupomacentrus	Pomacentrus

The Demoiselles are mostly small fishes and are to be found in all tropical seas in the shallows around reefs. Like Cichlids, to which they are closely related, they have one nostril on each side of the head. In fact many of their mannerisms are the same as their freshwater cousins. They are very territorial and defend their homes with the utmost ferocity. Some are found singly or in shoals above large coral heads, into which they quickly disappear when danger threatens, whilst others, the Clownfishes, live in the poisonous sea anemones with which they have a symbiotic relationship.

They settle down very well in an aquarium and are quite cheap and easy to obtain. Their adaptability makes them ideal for the beginner, but some are inclined to be scrappy amongst themselves, although seldom is any serious damage done. Dried food will be taken by most species but this should be supplemented with live food occasionally. If this is done they will live for quite a long time. The majority of members of this family are very highly coloured, ranging from red, through apple green, to violet.

Popular name: **Blue Devil**
Size: 3in (80mm)
Distribution: Philippines and throughout the Western Pacific

It has been suggested that this fish is merely an adult colour variation of the fish *Pomacentrus coeruleus* and, whilst the Latin name given here may not be strictly correct, I feel it should be placed under a different heading. To draw a comparison between the two: this particular fish lacks the dark spots at the dorsal base, whereas these are readily apparent on *P. coeruleus* also the blue extends to the tips of all the fins whilst this is not so on *P. coeruleus*. I find it hard to believe that all the specimens showing this particular colouration are not a distinct species, since the size of the fish may vary from ¾–2in (2–5mm). The only other explanation being that adulthood is reached at varying sizes, but I have yet to see a fish showing transitional colouration.

Popular name: as Latin name
Size: 4in (100mm)
Distribution: Red Sea, Indian and West Pacific Oceans

Though not often seen in this country this little Damsel is quite hardy and will feed happily on all usual flake and freeze-dried foods. It is not normally as pugnacious as other Damsels and can be kept in small groups without too much fin-nipping and bickering occuring.
A. biocellatus is a lively fish which is always on the move. It prefers the slightly higher temperature of between 78–82°F (25–27°C). It is common in its natural range but does not seem to be as popular as other members of this family.

Glyphidodontops cyaneus (Quoy & Gaimard)

Abudefduf biocellatus (Quoy & Gaimard)

Abudefduf hemicyaneus

Popular name: **Yellow-tailed Blue Damsel**
Size: 1¼in (32mm)
Distribution: Western Pacific Ocean

This fish is possibly the hardiest true marine fish. It can withstand most mistakes the beginner usually makes and will come back for more.

The difference in colouration between this species and that of *Pomacentrus melanochir* may not, at first, be apparent. The tails help to differentiate them. As can be seen from the photograph, this fish has the yellow starting well into the body and finishing just past the base of the caudal fin, leaving the tip of it relatively colourless.

Feeding, typical of most Damsels, presents no problem and flake food supplemented with occasional frozen shell-meat is ideal for this fish.

Abudefduf leucogaster (Bleeker)

Popular name: **Yellow Belly Devil**
Size: 6in (150mm)
Distribution: Western Pacific Ocean

This is not a very attractive fish and is, therefore, rarely seen in the shops. As an adult fish it is strongly territorial and becomes something of a problem for its owner. At this size it is a muddy colour with faint yellow tinges on the flanks.

Juvenile fish are more easy to handle and do quite well on a diet of flake food supplemented with fresh protein, such as shell-fish or tubifex.

Abudefduf oxyodon (Bleeker)

Popular name: **Neon Damsel** or **Blue Velvet Damsel**
Size: 4in (100mm)
Distribution: Malayan Archipelago, Philippines

A fish much revered by marine fishkeepers, the Blue Velvet Damsel is one of the most beautiful of a highly-coloured family.

This species is quite rare in the Indo-Pacific and even more so in the shops where, when it does appear, it is quite expensive compared with other Damselfish.

I remember one particular specimen I had that used to spend hours happily trying to 'worry' pieces of fresh shrimp that I suspended in the tank by a piece of cotton attached to the aquarium hood. The advantage of feeding fresh shrimp, etc in this manner is that it prevents large pieces of food being left on the aquarium floor, because any unwanted remains can simply be pulled out and thrown away.

Popular name: **Sergeant Major**
Size: 8in (200mm)
Distribution: Tropical Atlantic, Indo-Pacific, Red Sea

Almost as familiar in aquariums as on the reefs, the Sergeant Majors, as they are known by most aquarists, are one of the easiest coral fishes to keep. Despite their lack of attractive colours and their inherent aggressiveness these fishes enjoy considerable popularity amongst beginners. In their juvenile state they do not present a problem to the aquarist but as they grow older they become more boisterous, snappy and generally difficult.
They are good teachers where feeding is concerned, and will be first to the surface at feeding time, creating such a commotion that other non-feeders will soon follow their example.

Abudefduf saxatilis (Linnaeus)

Popular name: **Kupipi**
Size: 8in (200mm)
Distribution: Indo-West Pacific, Red Sea

The tail of this fish is not as deeply forked as that of *Abudefduf saxatilis*. Adult specimens are grey-blue in colour whilst the young fish are considerably darker.
The photograph here of a Solomon Island specimen shows quite clearly the six stripes which adorn the sides of the fish. A small black spot on the caudal peduncle further assists the aquarist in identification.
In an aquarium it is extremely hardy and is not in the least fussy about its food. It does become quite boisterous, though, and will cause its owner constant concern if housed with smaller and more reticent species. In spite of this I would recommend this species for the beginner providing care is taken in choosing suitable tank-mates.

Abudefduf sordidus (Forskal)   Photo: Dr Gerald R. Allen

Popular name: **Barrier Reef Anemonefish**
Size: 3½in (90mm)
Distribution: Eastern Australia to Loyalty Islands

This species is very similar in appearance to *Amphiprion chrysopterus*. It does, however, grow a little larger and is generally lighter in colouration. The juveniles are dark brown which lightens with age and have three white body bars. As a rule the adult fish has no third bar but it does have a completely white caudal fin.
It is another fish which is seldom seen in aquaria, but it should settle down to tank conditions as easily as other members of this group.

Amphiprion akindynos (Allen)

Amphiprion (Premnas) biaculeatus (Bloch)

Popular name : Premnas, Maroon Clownfish or Spine-cheeked Anemonefish
Size : 6in (150mm)
Distribution : Western Pacific to Mauritius

A slightly rarer species of Clownfish, it has been categorised into a separate sub-genus because of the sharp spine-like appendages on either side of the head.

These spines appear to be used as a defence mechanism and are capable of inflicting painful wounds on any would-be attacker. It is something of a loner and should not be kept with other species of Clownfishes, with which it can be quite nasty. Because of its relative scarcity it can be expensive, but it is easy to keep and feeding presents no problems.

When kept in an aquarium it does not appear to have the same affinity for anemones as most of its close relatives.

Amphiprion clarkii (Bennett)

Photo : Dr Gerald R. Allen

Popular name : Black Clown, Brown Anemonefish or Chocolate Clownfish
Size : 4½in (115mm)
Distribution : Tropical Western Pacific, Indian Ocean

This Clownfish is characterised by an orange belly and snout; the chocolate-brown background colouration on the sides becomes progressively darker with age.

It feeds well on flake food and freeze-dried varieties of most fresh proteins.

If no anemone is present, this species is inclined to be a little territorial and will get more belligerent as it reaches adulthood.

It is a lazy fish and spends most of its time motionless, but the first scent or sight of food will send it dashing around the aquarium trying to eat every morsel of food possible.

It is possible to breed this species and sexual maturity is attained at the age of approximately 18 months.

Popular name : Saddle Anemonefish
Size : 5in (130mm)
Distribution : Tropical Indo-Pacific

This species has a similar temperament to *A. frenatus*. In an aquarium it soon becomes strongly territorial and if several are kept together the largest specimen will pick on the next largest fish, being the strongest threat to its total dominance of the tank, who in turn will pick on the next smallest and so on down the line to the smallest specimen in the tank who will be picked on by everyone.

Feedings of frozen shell-meat or live shrimp will keep this fish in prime condition and this may be further supplemented with flake or freeze-dried foods.

Amphiprion ephippium (Bloch)

**Popular name: Fire Clown, Tomato Clown
or Red Clown**
Size: 5in (130mm)
Distribution: From Japan to Singapore and
the Philippine Islands

This Clownfish is somewhat more territorial
than other members of this genus, particularly
in its adult form. Some have the habit of
digging shallow depressions in the gravel by
rapid side-to-side movements of the tail, or by
shovelling gravel into the mouth, Cichlid
fashion. These pits are guarded with considerable ferocity, and this species will often nose
large pieces of coral around the tank when not
satisfied with their original position.
It is a friendly fish which will take dried foods
readily and live foods with even more relish.
Although rather susceptible to *Oodinium*, it
does quite well in captivity, with or without an
anemone to hide in, and may even be induced
to spawn.

Amphiprion frenatus (Brevoort)

Popular name: Wide-band Anemonefish
Size: minimum $4\frac{1}{2}$in (115mm)
Distribution: Northern New South Wales,
Lord Howe Island

Amphiprion latezonatus is very rare and is only
known from a handful of specimens at the
moment. The species came to light in 1900
and from then until 1971 was only known
from the single specimen collected. Since
1971, however, several more have been
discovered in Byron Bay, New South Wales.
I am grateful to Dr Gerald R. Allen for
supplying me with the photograph of a
Lord Howe Island specimen.
It is possible that specimens will eventually
show up in dealers' tanks despite their present
rarity. It is easily distinguished from other
species by the unusual caudal pattern and
broad mid-body band, which is much wider
than that of any other Clownfishes.

Amphiprion latezonatus (Waite)   Photo: Dr Gerald R. Allen

Popular name: Fire Clown
Size: 4in (100mm)
Distribution: Polynesia, Melanesia, Micronesia,
Australia

This fish can be identified as a separate
species from *A. mccullochi* by the headband
being connected mid-dorsally. in *A. mccullochi*
this band usually terminates well before the
top of the head. In addition to this the caudal
fin of *A. melanopus* is much more rounded.
A further confusion often occurs when the
species *Amphiprion rubrocinctus* is
encountered. This latter species, though, has
much paler pelvic fins than *A. melanopus*.
All fishes of the 'ephippium group' are easy to
keep and seldom prove demanding to the
experienced aquarist. Feeding and care is as
for others of this genus.

Amphiprion melanopus (Bleeker)   Photo: Dr Gerald R. Allen

Amphiprion ocellaris (Cuvier)

Popular name: **Clown Anemonefish** or
Common Clown
Size: 8in (200mm)
Distribution: Tropical Indo-Pacific

This Clown makes an enchanting addition to a
community tank. It takes dried foods readily
and soon settles down to aquarium life with
or without an anemone host.

I think, personally, it is unfortunate that such a
beautifully coloured fish should be named
Common Clown; I myself prefer to call it the
Clown Anemonefish.

It can be induced to spawn (see chapter on
breeding) and the eggs hatch after seven to
eight days. The young fry are pelagic for about
fourteen days, after which they settle to the
bottom in search of an anemone host.
A. ocellaris can be differentiated from the
similar A. percula by ray counts of the dorsal
fins. A. ocellaris has eleven dorsal spines
whereas A. percula has normally only ten.

Amphiprion perideraion (Bleeker)   Photo: Bruce Coleman

Popular name: **Pink Skunk Clown, White-
banded Anemonefish** or **False Skunk-
striped Anemonefish**
Size: 3¼in (85mm)
Distribution: Central and Western Pacific Ocean

Feeding can present a problem at first due to
their reticence. However, if after introduction
into a tank the lights are left off until the
following morning, then the following evening
when their first food is offered they usually take it.
This species can be bred and prior to spawning
the male and female prepare the nest site.
Active courtship ensues and, after spawning,
it is the male who cares for the eggs. After six
or seven days they hatch and the fry are ⅛in
(4mm) long at this stage. After a further seven
days they will have almost doubled their size
and colouration begins to show. It is at this
stage that they settle to the bottom and look
for an anemone in which to live.

Amphiprion polymnus (Linnaeus)   Photo: Dr Gerald R. Allen

Popular name: **Saddle-back Clown**
Size: 5in
Distribution: Western Pacific Ocean

The arrow-shaped caudal pattern helps to
differentiate this species from A. sebae, which
has a pale caudal fin. The basic body
colouration of the Saddle-back Clown can
vary from mid-brown to black and the area
covered by the mid-body band can also vary
in size. Occasionally a third bar may be found
on the caudal base, though this is seldom seen.
This species is often imported from the
Philippines and is ideal for a community tank.
If possible it should be kept with an anemone,
though this is not a necessity.

Normally this fish will live on a diet of all the
usual fresh and dried aquarium foods, though
occasional specimens will prove to be
exceptions to this rule and should be taught to
feed on brine shrimp initially and subsequently
weaned onto freeze-dried foods.

Popular name: **Yellow Skunk Clown**
Size: 3½in (90mm)
Distribution: Philippines, New Guinea to Solomon Islands

This species is often confused with *A. akallopisos*. *A. sandaracinos* has the white band extending onto the upper lip, otherwise the overall body colour is identical, both species having yellow on the belly and fins. It is a hardy fish and will take the first food an hour or so after introduction. If an anemone host is present it will usually form a symbiotic relationship with it far more quickly than other members of this genus.

It is quite an experience seeing this phenomenon for the first time and I still find it enchanting even now. To see the way that this fish snuggles into its anemone with complete impunity is an unforgettable experience.

Amphiprion sandaracinos (Allen)

Photo: Dr Gerald R. Allen

Popular name: **Sebae Clown** or **Brown Clown**
Size: 5in (130mm)
Distribution: Indian Ocean to Java

The Sebae Clown is similar in appearance to *Amphiprion polymnus* but has a pale caudal fin and caudal peduncle, whereas *A. polymnus* has a much darker tail region. The mid-body bar of this fish, unlike its close cousin, is almost complete at the belly.

It is a frequently imported species that does well in captivity. Its diet is varied and this means that it will accept most of the foods that are offered. As it grows it will get more pugnacious so the aquarist should make allowances for this when choosing its tank-mates. If a large *Radianthus* anemone is included in its tank it will happily demonstrate that it has the ability to live unharmed amongst the tentacles.

Amphiprion sebae (Bleeker)

Popular name: **Maroon Clown**
Size: 4in (100mm)
Distribution: Marshall Islands

This fish normally has three white bands circling the body. The background colouration may vary considerably from orange to black. It is a deep-bodied fish and is quite common within its natural range.

In an aquarium it is normally a placid species, although occasionally an adult will prove to be over-boisterous with its smaller tank-mates; this is usually due to territorial squabbles and seldom is it serious or damaging. Most fights of this nature can be solved by the use of a larger tank. When this is not possible more cover and hiding places, constructed from rocks and corals, should be provided for both the troublesome and troubled.

Amphiprion tricinctus (Schultz & Welander)

Chromis caeruleus (Cuvier & Valenciennes)

Popular name: **Green Chromis** or **Blue-green Chromis**
Size: 3in (75mm)
Distribution: Indo-West Pacific, Red Sea

A well known favourite with many aquarists, it is an inexpensive fish and ideal for the beginner because of its hardiness.

The striking colour, a metallic apple-green, makes it easily identifiable and a dozen or so kept in a 25 gallon (115 litre) tank will make an attractive display. In a community tank this fish tends to be a fin-nipper so care should be taken to avoid this.

As with all Damsels, food is no problem and will usually be accepted an hour or so after the fish has been introduced into the tank.

Chromis cyanea (Poey)

Popular name: **Blue Chromis** or **Blue-forked Tail Damsel**
Size: 4in (100mm)
Distribution: Tropical Western Atlantic

This is a very attractive fish and can be found in the shallows of the reefs, sometimes in shoals. The tail is deeply forked and the dorsal is tipped with black. The remainder of the body is deep iridescent blue in colour.

They are quite mild-mannered fishes and nothing is more pleasing to the eye than a small shoal of them darting back and forth over an artistically created coral 'reef' in one's living room. A dozen or so will live happily in a 60 gallon (270 litre) tank.

Feeding presents no problem and all the better quality dried foods will be eagerly accepted, but dried food alone will not be sufficient and should be supplemented with frozen shell-meat.

Dascyllus aruanus (Linnaeus)

Popular name: **Humbug Damsel, Black and White Damsel** or **White-tailed Damselfish**
Size: 3in (75mm)
Distribution: Indo-West Pacific, Red Sea

This is a popular fish for the marine aquarium, especially with beginners. The Humbug Damsel is very hardy and can stand quite high nitrite levels seemingly with no ill-effects. It has a wide diet and will eat anything and everything that is offered. Whilst being a good beginners' fish, it is strongly territorial and this can sometimes pose a few problems when choosing its tank-mates. A little forethought and frequent reference to this book will save quite a few nipped and split fins and get the would-be marine aquarist off to a good start. Plenty of coral heads should be provided for this fish and nothing looks more attractive than a shoal of a dozen or so creatures in a well furnished 40 gallon (180 litre) tank.

Popular name: **Cloudy Damselfish,
Freckled Damselfish, White-tailed
Dascyllus** or **Blue-top Damselfish**
Size: 3in (75mm)
Distribution: Indian Ocean

This fish is ideal for the novice, being
extremely hardy and easy to keep. It is very
undemanding in its food requirements.
Apart from the usual dried foods you should
feed this Damselfish tubifex or brine shrimp on
a weekly basis to keep it in prime condition.

Dascyllus carneus (Fischer)

Popular name: **Four-striped Damsel,
Black-tailed Dascyllus** or **Black-tailed
Humbug**
Size: 3in (75mm)
Distribution: Indo-Pacific Ocean

This species is similar in appearance to *D.
aruanus*. It is generally less 'scrappy', although
just as hardy. If a dozen or so specimens are
well presented in an aquarium of at least 30
gallons (135 litres), little can touch them for
natural beauty. A set-up like this allows the
fish to shoal, providing the aquarium is not too
large and does not contain holes and crevices
which would make them territorially aggressive.
All Damselfishes show territorial tendencies,
but if the fishes are housed in a tank large
enough to avoid overcrowding but small
enough to prevent them establishing territorial
rights then the problem can be overcome.

Dascyllus melanurus (Bleeker)

Popular name: **Three-spot Damsel** or
Domino Damsel
Size: 4½in (115mm)
Distribution: Red Sea, Indian and Western
Pacific Oceans

A somewhat pugnacious fish but quite
attractive all the same. It looks better in the
company of others of the same species due to
its shoaling nature. The young specimen is jet
black with white, almost luminous spots, one
on each flank and one on the forehead.
However, as they grow older the black
becomes more grey and the spots fade slightly.
The Domino is a good fish for the beginner
because of its wide appetite. It feeds well on a
diet of dried foods and occasional fresh
chopped shrimp. It is quite hardy and will live
for years, although adult fish are usually
aggressively territorial.
They have been bred in captivity, although
infrequently.

Dascyllus trimaculatus (Rüppell)

Glyphidodontops hemicyaneus

Photo: Dr Gerald R. Allen

Popular name: **Bicolor Damsel**
Size: 2in (50mm)
Distribution: New Guinea

This is a startling fish which, in my opinion, is the most beautiful of all the Damselfishes. It is not very often available, but when it is imported it is usually sold immediately. Perhaps the professional collectors will be able to find a good supply of these fishes in the near future for they are ideally suited to aquarium life, being only 2in (50mm) in total length when fully grown.

Feeding and care of the Bicolor Damsel is the same as for other members of this family.

Neopomacentrus azysron

Photo: Dr Gerald R. Allen

Popular name: as Latin name
Size: 3in (75mm)
Distribution: Melanesia to the Philippines

This fish is similar in appearance to *Pomacentrus melanochir,* although not quite as colourful. It is also much rarer but may occasionally appear in dealers' tanks. Unfortunately, professional collectors tend to overlook species like this and go for similar, but much more colourful, specimens with the result that they only appear in the shops by accident.

Popular name: **Black and Gold Damsel**
Size: 3in (75mm)
Distribution: Tropical Western Pacific Ocean

Most Damselfishes, with the exception of the genus *Paraglyphidodon,* retain more or less the same colour pattern throughout their lives. With this particular species the young are completely different from the adult fish, being an overall dull yellow with purplish tinges and two distinct horizontal bars running down the sides of the fish. A comparison can be made by studying the two photographs.

The young fish are ideal for a marine aquarium, but as they get older they become more scrappy to a point where it can be a serious problem. Feeding them is easy, though, and they will take most of the conventional aquarium foods. They should, however, be given an occasional treat of shell-meat such as squid or chopped clam.

Photo: Dr Gerald R. Allen

The young P. behni shown here is a far more attractive fish than its adult version.

Paraglyphidodon behni

Popular name: **Bowtie Damsel** or **Blue Fin Damsel**
Size: 3in (75mm)
Distribution: Tropical Indo-West Pacific

A very attractive Damselfish which is not too aggressive for a community set-up. It does not seem to be as hardy as most other members of this family and is often imported with various viral infections. These can be eradicated quite easily by quarantine and one of the wide range of cures available for this type of ailment. This fish is a hearty feeder, accepting most aquarium dried foods, though it should be remembered that there is no substitute for live foods and even Damselfishes need an occasional treat to keep them in top condition.

Paraglyphidodon melanopus

Photo: Dr Gerald R. Allen

Pomacentrus amboinensis (Bleeker)

Popular name: **Yellow Damsel**
Size: 4in (100mm)
Distribution: Tropical West Pacific

The Yellow Damsel, when young, presents no problem to the marine aquarist. Moreover, it is a colourful fish, being bright yellow, and is a popular choice for a community set-up. Larger specimens are a different matter, since they become territorial and scrappy. They also have a habit of making a mess of an otherwise attractive tank by digging holes and pits. Their food requirements are varied but feeding is made easy by their natural habit of attempting to swallow everything that even remotely looks like food. General care is the same as for other members of this family.

Pomacentrus coeruleus (Quoy & Gaimard)

Popular name: **Electric Blue Damselfish** or **Blue Devil**
Size: 2½in (65mm)
Distribution: Central and Western Pacific Ocean

Often stated to be a beginners fish, but I would venture to disagree with this statement. Young specimens are inclined to be a bit scrappy amongst themselves and other Damsels, and as they get older they become pugnacious and territorial. Usually, one finds they will stake out a claim for a particular crevice they have made and its surrounding area, and ferociously protect this claim much to the dismay of any small fish chancing to pass by it. This can sometimes present more of a problem to the aquarist than, say, trying to get some obscure species of Butterflyfish to feed properly.
Provided a suitable choice of tank-mates is made—for example, small Triggerfish—then the aquarist will have little trouble.

Pomacentrus melanochir (Bleeker)

Popular name: **Yellow-tailed Blue Damsel** or **Saffron Blue Damsel**
Size: 4in (100mm)
Distribution: Sri Lanka, Indo-Pacific

This Damsel has enjoyed popularity for many years now. It is an unassuming fish that is a firm favourite of mine. Although it can grow quite large for a Damsel, I have never found this species quite so pugnacious as other books would have them.
They certainly add colour to an aquarium and are quite easily pleased as far as food is concerned, taking flake and freeze-dried food with relish.
Occasionally a specimen may dig pits in the gravel and this can possibly lead to problems if the operating efficiency of the undergravel filter is impaired by being exposed. Apart from this, it is an ideal aquarium fish.

Sciaenidae (Drums or Croakers)

Genus: Equetus

Some of the larger members of this family grow to 3ft (900mm) in length. Because of this, one normally finds only smaller representatives from this genus in marine aquaria.

The Drums are to be found in both tropical and sub-tropical seas, usually near the coastline. They are essentially bottom-feeders. They have two dorsal fins; the anterior one is normally much higher than the posterior one, the two being slightly connected.

The common names—Drum or Croaker—come from their ability to make loud underwater noises, particularly when they are in shoals. These sounds are produced by muscle contractions which make the swim bladder vibrate.

Popular name: **Cubbyu** or **High-hat**
Size: 9½in (240mm)
Distribution: Tropical Western Atlantic

Though well known by most aquarists, this fish is seldom kept with much success. It is a timid species and consequently very prone to shock. If correctly introduced, however, the Cubbyu has the ability to thrive in captivity and, under optimum conditions, there is always a chance that spawning and subsequent raising of young may be possible. I have found that a diet of chopped shrimp and crab is sufficient to keep the Cubbyu in a healthy condition. This is not to say, though, that the aquarist should not try and experiment with foods of a similar nature.

Equetus acuminatus (Bloch & Schneider)

120

Scorpionfishes inhabit all seas, but the tropical species are more exotic, having longer rays on their fins. Generally they are bottom-dwellers and spend most of their time amongst rocks stalking small fishes for food. Occasionally they are found upside-down underneath an overhanging, submerged rock. Some 'walk' on their extended pectoral fins along the bottom. They all have large mouths for their size and are masters of disguise. They are also extremely dangerous and inflict painful wounds on divers and swimmers by means of their hollow, poisonous dorsal and opercular spines. In captivity they should become tame but must still be handled with extreme caution.

Colouration is of a streaky, dappled nature and they have the ability to change this in a matter of seconds. They are very lazy fishes, preferring the food to come to them rather than hunting it down. Peculiar though this trait is, they make good community fish if kept well supplied with live food and pieces of shell-meat. Care should also be taken to ensure that tank-mates of a Scorpionfish are of a similar size.

Scorpaenidae (Scorpionfishes)

Including the following genera:
Dendrochirus   Pterois
Parapterois

Pterois volitans (Linnaeus)   Photo: Bruce Coleman

Popular name: **Dwarf Lionfish** or **Zebra Lionfish**
Size: 8in (200mm)
Distribution: Indian and Pacific Oceans

These days, the import consignments contain more and more of this particular species. It is popular because of its small size when compared with other Lionfishes. It is quite attractive too, having enormous pectoral fins. It thrives well in an aquarium and is particularly fond of guppies as live food. Small Clownfishes are also often devoured, so be careful where you house it! These fish, along with others of this family, are predators and therefore cannot be blamed for following their natural instincts.

Dendrochirus zebra (Quoy & Gaimard)

Popular name: **Spotfin Lionfish**
Size: 8in (200mm)
Distribution: Red Sea, Indian and Pacific Oceans

This beautiful Scorpionfish, or Lionfish as it is sometimes called, is my own personal favourite among a truly bizarre family. As the popular name implies, the long flowing pectoral fins are liberally covered with large spots on the wide membranes which stretch between the individual fin rays.

It is quite common to see this particular fish on the reefs of the Indo-Pacific. It can be found in caves and grottos swimming upside down against the roofs of its rocky haven.

A similar fish, and one which often causes taxonomic confusion, is *Pterois sphex,* the range of which is restricted to the Hawaiian Islands.

Pterois antennata (Bloch)

Pterois lunulata (Temminck & Schlegel)

Popular name: **Scorpionfish**
Size: 14in (360mm)
Distribution: Indo-Pacific

The main points that help to differentiate this fish from *Pterois volitans*, its closest relative, are the lack of supraorbital tentacles and slight differences in colour.

It can be seen that there are long feather-like protuberances above the eyes of *P. volitans* which are not present with this species. The second point is less distinct, but the colour of *P. lunulata* appears much brighter and more reddish.

Despite these differences all Scorpionfishes have the same basic feeding habits and, although nocturnal by nature, will feed quite happily during daytime hours. This does not imply that they are any less active at night.

Pterois volitans (Linnaeus)

Photo: Dr Gerald R. Allen

Popular name: **Peacock Lionfish, Scorpionfish, Turkeyfish** or **Butterfly Cod**
Size: 14in (360mm)
Distribution: Indo-Pacific, Red Sea

By far the most common and popular Lionfish, it is just as colourful as any other and its poisonous spines are just as potent.

There is no group more placid than the Lionfishes. Admittedly they can be deadly to both humans and to the small fishes they will quickly eat if placed in the same tank, but on the whole they behave themselves and are quite mild-mannered creatures given the correct living conditions. In fact, they could even be classed as beginners' fish, providing the beginner uses his head and caters sensibly for their requirements and his own safety. This species is extremely hardy and will provide its owner with many happy hours. It feeds well on a diet of fresh protein and many even take dried foods.

Syngnathidae
(Sea Horses and Pipefishes)

Including the following genera:

Entelurus	Syngnathus
Hippocampus	Dunkerocampus

Sea Horses are widespread in most tropical and temperate seas. They have bony external skeletons and long prehensile tails with which they anchor themselves to the coral. They propel their bodies through the water by rapid undulations of their dorsal fins. Even so, they are quite slow moving and are often beaten to the post where food is concerned. For this reason they should either be kept with small peaceful fishes or housed in a tank of their own. This should be furnished with plenty of corals, preferably the branch variety or, better still, sea whips. This provides them with hitching posts on to which they can anchor their tails.

They are rather fastidious in their requirements, needing plenty of light, aeration and live foods. Because of this they are rather difficult to keep, but well worth the trouble.

Pipefishes, which belong to the same family, are also slow moving and consequently make good tank-mates for the Sea Horses. The beginner would do better to stay clear of this family, though, until he has gained experience with some hardier species.

Popular name: **Zebra Pipefish**
Size: 6in (150mm)
Distribution: Indo-Australian Archipelago

This is the most attractive of all the Pipefishes and can be identified relatively easily. Colouration consists of a pale background circled with 20 to 30 brownish-black bands. The body is long and slender with a prominent snout. This is used for picking tiny food particles and crustaceans from the sea-bed. In an aquarium Pipefishes are difficult to feed but will accept newly hatched brine shrimp. There is a possibility that this fish may be bred in captivity though, at the moment, I know of no reports to substantiate this.

Like the Sea Horses, it is the male that has the brood pouch in which the young are incubated.

Dunkerocampus dactyliophorus (Bleeker)

opposite: **Hippocampus hudsonius** (De Kay)

Popular name: **Short-snouted Sea Horse**
Size: 8in (200mm)
Distribution: Mediterranean and East Atlantic

Sea Horses such as this species require an all-year-round supply of live food and this may pose quite a problem for the aquarist. If, however, a small tank is set to one side purely for breeding and rearing guppies for food or hatching brine shrimp then the job of feeding is made considerably easier.

I feel it should be pointed out here that whilst Sea Horses are charming and relatively cheap, they are definitely not for the beginner. I have seen many experienced aquarists fail to keep these fishes for more than a few weeks (their natural life-span is sometimes as much as three years).

Hippocampus brevirostris (Cuvier)

Popular name: **Atlantic Sea Horse** or **Northern Sea Horse**
Size: 10in (250mm)
Distribution: Tropical West Atlantic

This fish grows quite large. Colouration is similar to that of *Hippocampus hippocampus,* though this fish lacks the long tubercles along its back and on its head.

As with all Sea Horses it must be kept in a tank of its own rather than in a community set-up. This is because it is too slow moving to be able to compete for food with the more boisterous fishes. A separate aquarium of about 20 gallons (90 litres) containing various Pipefishes and Sea Horses is the best method of keeping members of this family.

Hippocampus hudsonius (De Kay)

Popular name: **Yellow Sea Horse** or **Oceanic Sea Horse**
Size: 10in (250mm)
Distribution: Indo-Pacific

The most popular of all the members of this family and the one most often offered for sale in dealers' tanks.

In an aquarium it is quiet and undemanding and needs to be provided with a plentiful supply of live food, such as bloodworms, tubifex or brine shrimps. The aquarium furnishings should consist mainly of branch coral and sea whips around which it can wrap its characteristic prehensile tail.

Substantiated reports of this fish breeding within the confines of an aquarium are not uncommon and I recommend that they should be bought in pairs instead of singly so that the aquarist can try his hand at breeding them. The young require to be fed as often as is practical on newly hatched brine shrimp.

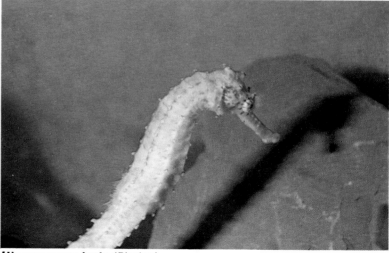

Hippocampus kuda (Bleeker)

Only one genus represents this last family. Throughout the tropical Indo-Pacific there is one fish which stands out from all the others and that is the Moorish Idol. It is rather difficult to keep alive, though, and possibly too expensive to lose.

Zanclidae are related to both the Butterflyfishes and the Tangs and lie, taxonomically speaking, midway between these two families. They are, therefore, often confused with the similar looking members of the genus *Heniochus* by the more inexperienced aquarist. Closer observation reveals a strongly compressed body adorned with small scales. They have a protruding snout and a rather small mouth, but the most obvious feature is the elongated third ray of the dorsal fin which, in some specimens, arcs high over the body past the tail.

On the reefs these fish are to be found in small shoals around coral heads browsing on the minute organisms that form the staple part of their diet. Getting them to feed regularly in captivity, though, is no easy task.

Zanclidae (Moorish Idols)

Genus: Zanclus

Zanclus canescens (Linnaeus)

Popular name: Zanclus, Moorish Idol or Toby
Size: 10in (250mm)
Distribution: Indian Ocean to Central Pacific

Very choosy about its diet and difficult to keep—this fish is for the experienced aquarist only—the *Zanclus* is a strikingly graceful fish and one of nature's wonders.

It is not a rare fish by any means and is usually found in shoals. The difficulty in keeping specimens alive long enough to get them to the shops is what determines their fairly high price.

Behavioural characteristics

Right: Chaetodon lunula showing signs of shock has found a place to hide between two pieces of coral that its thoughtful owner has provided on its initial introduction to the tank to facilitate a more speedy recovery. *Below: Chaetodon chrysurus,* the Pearl-scaled Butterflyfish is seen here shortly after initial introduction to an aquarium and exhibits typical symptoms of shock i.e. 'Hugging' the corner of the tank, body resting on the gravel, slight loss of colour this being accompanied by an increase in respiratory rate (gill movement).

Both these Damselfishes are exhibiting the behaviour pattern of a vigorously territorial fish. (Note the body angle and darkened colours). From this fairly stationary position they are able to dart out at any fish that comes too close and chase it away. At the same time they are able to retire into the coral closeby if any real danger is present.

Both these fishes: *Oxycirrhites typus,* the Long Nosed Hawkfish and *Synchiropus splendidus,* the Mandarin Fish, are using their pelvic fins to 'perch' on the coral. This trait is normally exhibited by members of the Goby family but, as can be seen here, Hawkfishes and Dragonets do the same sometimes.

Part 3 Invertebrates

Plexaura flexuosa, shown above, lacks the highly branched composition of the Gorgonid Sea Fans and is classified as a Sea Whip

Radianthus malu

Radianthus ritteri

Edwardsia sp

Cnidopus verater

Invertebrates
(animals without backbones)

There are perhaps a million different species of invertebrates on this planet, many of which live in the sea; it would take a double lifetime for one man to classify and write about them. What I have tried to do here is to select an assortment of creatures which the reader will stand a good chance of seeing during his travels to the pet-shop or the sea.

Most invertebrates are fairly undemanding creatures which any marine aquarist with a little experience can keep and enjoy. Many advanced marine aquarists have gone so far as to develop tanks for invertebrates only, in which an assortment of creatures live and propagate, making a true living reef in their living room.

To be practical I have only included seven of the twenty-five phyla in this chapter. This is because the aquarist will seldom have anything to do with the other eighteen phyla; these being of little interest or importance to him.

Listed below are the seven phyla of interest to the aquarist:

1 Phylum-Protozoa   One-celled animals
2 Phylum-Porifera   The Sponges
3 Phylum-Cnidaria   Hydroids, Jellyfishes, Sea Anemones, Corals
4 Phylum-Echino-dermata   Starfish, Sea Urchins, Sea Cucumbers
5 Phylum Annelida   Segmented Sea Worms, Feather Duster Worms
6 Phylum-Arthro-poda   Horseshoe Crabs, Crustaceans
7 Phylum-Mollusca   Molluscs

1 Phylum-Protozoa

These one-celled animals are too microscopic to be seen with the naked eye. However, the aquarist should be aware of the fact that proto-zoans, such as the parasitic *Dinoflagellates,* are often responsible for the deaths of fishes in aquaria. In the sea the weird luminescent 'night-light' on the tops of waves is caused by a great number of *Dinoflagellates* called *Noctil-uca* which are just one of the many types of marine creatures that possess luminescence.

2 Phylum-Porifera (the Sponges)

It would be an impossible task to try to describe all the different species of sponges because, due to water conditions, they vary in size, shape and colour so drastically. For instance, one may be yellow and cup-shaped, about 5in (130mm) high, whilst another, violet, fan-like and 10in (250mm) high, and yet they could be the same species! A few may be identified by examining their skeletons.

Sponges are filter-feeders and may be kept alive in aquaria given optimum water conditions. Water is drawn in through the thousands of pores in the body, along with microscopic food forms, which are then separated from the water, which is subsequently expelled through the many larger openings. They are plant-like creatures which remain fixed in one place for life.

Reproduction may be by the depositing of spores in the water, which settle and in time form new sponges, or by 'separation', where a number of cells branch out from the main body to eventually become separated and thereby form a new sponge. There is nothing to stop the aquarist from artificially reproducing them by clipping off a portion and allowing it to settle and attach itself to a rock where it will, in time, become another sponge. This taking of 'cutt-ings' is often practised by sponge farmers to increase their yield.

3 Phylum-Cnidaria (Hydras, Jellyfishes, Corals and Sea Anemones)

There are about 10,000 species of Cnidarian animals and these are split into three classes as follows:

Hydrozoa—Jellyfishes and Hydras

Scyphozoa—True Jellyfishes

Anthozoa—Sea Fans, Whips, Anemones and Corals

Of these three classes only the animals of the class Anthozoa are of interest to the marine aquarist, although occasionally Jellyfishes from the class Scyphozoa make their appearance in shop tanks.

Goniopora Coral, *Phylum cnidaria*

Sea Fans and Whips

These are *alcyonarians* or soft corals and, along with other forms of soft coral, they are becoming more frequently available to the aquarist. Both the Sea Fans and the Whips are comprised of a soft springy, stick-like skeleton covered with a layer of soft tissue. The latter may be highly coloured and contains the polyps, which are often of a contrasting colour.

Anemones

Anemones may be considered as much larger versions of the minute coral polyps in as much as they also lack an anus but have a radial symmetry and an oral disc surrounded by tentacles. Broadly speaking, the anemone can be split into three parts: the oral disc, the main body stem or column and the pedal disc or base.

The tentacles surrounding the oral disc are normally equipped with cnidoblasts or nemato-

cysts, which are tiny stinging cells. These cells are used for defence, and also in an offensive role to capture and hold prey.

Anemones come in a variety of shapes and sizes, all of which may be kept in an aquarium. The most frequently available ones are of the following genera:

Actinia	Discosoma
Anemonia	Oulactis
Anthopleura	Physobrachia
Cerianthus	Radianthus
Cnidopus	Stoichactis
Condylactis	Tealia

Apart from the cylinder or tube anemones of the order *Ceriantharia*, the encrusting sea anemones of the order *Zoantharia* and the family *Gonactiniidae*, all the anemones we see in aquaria belong to the same suborder—*Nynantheae*. The preceding photographs show a few

Cerianthus sp

Bubble Coral (*Plyrogyra sp*)

Orange Coral (*Tubastria aurea*)

The Feather Duster Worm (*Sabella sp*)

The Banded Coral Shrimp (*Stenopus hispidus*)

The Red-lined Shrimp (*Lysmata grabhami*)
Photograph by Keith Foskett

of the thousand or so species comprising this suborder which are available to marine aquarists.

Cylinder or tube anemones of the order *Ceriantharia* are separable from most other anemones by their lack of a pedal disc. They are burrowing anemones and therefore the presence of a pedal disc is not required. A tube is built around the column and consists of mud or sand, bits of shell and other debris bound together with a form of mucous secreted by the anemone.

Normally the tentacles are much longer and more potent than in other anemones and, whilst most anemones are easy to keep in an aquarium, members of this order will tend to migrate out of their tubes and die if the water conditions are anything but perfect.

Corals

Most corals can be kept in an aquarium and the vast majority of them do quite well when they are kept under the correct conditions. For instance, it is no good expecting them to thrive in a newly set-up aquarium since it is essential that their environment is well matured. Moreover, they can be expected to die if there is a presence of nitrite in their tank. Further to this, they do seem to fare much better if a partial water change is carried out at regular intervals and when plenty of aeration is present. There are many hardy types available these days which seem to require not quite so strict water management.

4 Phylum-Echinodermata (Starfish, Sea Urchins and Sea Cucumbers)

Members of this phylum are also radial animals having five segments, however vague this may appear at first glance. The majority of them are also spiny-skinned creatures, hence the name Echinoderm. This is derived from the Greek *echinos* for hedgehog and *derma* meaning skin.

There are five classes which make up the main part of this phylum and they are as follows:

Crinoidea—Crinoids
Asteroidea—Sea Stars
Ophiuroidea—Brittle and Basket Stars
Echinoidea—Sea Urchins and Sand Dollars
Holothuroidea—Sea Cucumbers

Crinoidea

These are often referred to as sea lilies or feather stars. They are not often seen, since most of them come from the great depths of the oceans. Even so they occasionally appear on dealers' lists, but are soon snapped up by collectors and aquarists alike because of their great beauty. Feather stars are known to have existed for millions of years from the thousands of fossilised species known to man. In an aquarium they generally appear to be reasonably hardy and usually do quite well. Perhaps this hardiness is the reason why they have been around for so long.

Asteroidea

The Sea Stars are among the most commonly seen invertebrates in aquaria. The body consists of a central 'hub' with five arms radiating from it. These arms may be short and stubby or long and slender. Sometimes there may be more than five arms, as in the 'Crown-of-Thorns' Starfish (*Acanthaster planci*) which are known to have up to twenty-three arms. The mouth of the starfish is situated on the underside in the central part of the 'hub'. Radiating outwards from this are the numerous tiny legs, or 'tube feet' as they are sometimes known. These are moved independently and are used to propel the starfish over any surface no matter how smooth.

Ophiuroidea

The Brittle and Basket Stars are not often seen in aquaria because of their shy and retiring nature. In the daytime they prefer to hide under rocks and corals, coming out only at night to forage for food. For this reason they are of little interest to the aquarist.

Brittle Stars, as the name implies, are extremely fragile and will shed their arms if they are handled too roughly. Their bodies are quite small, up to 1in (25mm) in diameter, but their arms often exceed 12in (300mm) in length. Some of the Brittle Stars are brightly coloured and all are relatively inexpensive.

Basket Stars look remarkably like plants at first glance, having arms which branch out in a complex manner, somewhat similar in fact to the fern-like structure of some plants. In an aquarium they are slow-moving creatures with a semi-sessile existence, although they appear to be quite hardy.

Echinoidea

Sand Dollars, small circular animals with tiny 'tube feet' and soft spines, are of little interest to the aquarist since they tend to spend most of their time buried in the sand at the bottom of the tank. Even so they are quite attractive and have a five-armed star embossed on their upper surface.

The major part of this suborder is made up of Sea Urchins which are well known as prickly animals whose skeletons are often sold as ornaments. Their spines may be quite long, up to about 1ft (300mm) in length, or they may be so short as to be almost unnoticeable. The body is enclosed in a spherical shell which is flattened on the underside. The mouth, sometimes referred to as 'Aristotle's Lantern', is also on the underside and consists of five teeth-like structures which open and close together in a 'rasping' manner.

In an aquarium the Sea Urchins have proved to be very hardy and will withstand relatively high nitrite levels. They prefer living rock in their tank and will spend a great deal of their time browsing on this. The aquarist should be warned, though, that it would be folly to house one in a tank of expensive lower order invertebrates and algae, since it would soon make short work of them.

Holothuroidea

Sea Cucumbers, or Sea Apples as they are sometimes called, are another popular type of invertebrate animal. They are slow moving though and, I think, rather dull additions to an aquarium. Their bodies are spongy, often highly coloured, with a series of plume-like appendages at one end to attract and capture food. These can be withdrawn into the body when the animal is not feeding. Waste matter is expelled at the opposite end.

They require no special treatment in an aquarium providing the water is well matured and will usually derive sufficient nourishment from the uneaten food present in any semi-natural system. However, liquid fry food and food intended for the filter feeding invertebrates may be used to supplement this.

5 Phylum-Annelida (Segmented Sea Worms)

The most well-known group of animals from this phylum is the group known as the Feather Duster Worms. These creatures live in tubes singly or in colonies and are characterised by their colourful feather-like gill filaments. It is remarkable that these creatures should have adapted their gills into such a complex structure. Normally, the worm will spread its feathery plumes outside its tube in order to trap food particles. If it is successful, or if danger threatens, it will draw itself back into its tube so quickly that the movement is almost imperceptible.

Apart from the relatively large types, like the one shown above, there are many smaller ones which can sometimes be seen on pieces of living rock. These may be only 1–2mm long.

Other Annelids include the Sea Mouse, which is really a worm that has evolved with a short oval-shaped body, and the many types of Clamworms, which are much more worm-like, often poisonous, and on the whole of little interest to the marine aquarist.

6 Phylum-Arthropoda (Joint-legged animals)

Although there are almost a million different species in this, the largest of all the phyla (most of which are land-dwelling insects), we are only concerned with a relatively small group, or class, called *Crustacea*. This class embodies all the crayfish, shrimps, lobsters, crabs and barnacles of the world.

A selection of four Sea Stars from the Indo-Pacific. These and others are readily available in the shops

The sucker-like feet of a Sea Star can be clearly seen here along with the central oral opening

The Long-spined Sea Urchin (*Diadema savignyi*) much sought- after by aquarists

Crustacea

Horseshoe Crab, *Phylum anthropoda*

There is an abundant variety of crustaceans suitable for the marine aquarium and many of them are highly coloured. It is probable that the beginner's first experience with invertebrates will be with a member of this particular class. Most of them are scavengers and are therefore of great value to the aquarist in that they will eat any abandoned food which may otherwise pollute the tank water.

Shrimps, like the ones illustrated, and Hermit Crabs seem to have more appeal than their larger cousins, the crabs and lobsters. The Fiddler Crab, however, is an exception to this rule and retains its popularity in spite of its pugnacious nature.

One of the more bizarre aspects of keeping crustaceans is their periodic 'shedding' of their shells. Usually the discarded shell is left as a perfect image of the animal that has just left it. Even the feelers, which may be quite long, are left attached to their shell in the natural position. Frequently this leads one to believe that there

are two animals instead of only one. Of course, once the shell is disturbed it will usually fall apart, but some of the larger species, like the Spiny Lobster, whose shell is fairly strong, can produce a shell that may be dried and varnished. They make excellent ornaments.

7 Phylum-Mollusca

Cephalopods

This group includes the octopuses and squids which, although often offered for sale, do not make good tank inhabitants. The octopuses in particular are expert escapologists and will climb out of the tank unless a secure cover glass is fitted. They appear not to adapt to aquarium life and will sometimes succumb for no apparent reason. In general, they require optimum tank conditions and even then there is only a limited chance of success.

Their aquarium should be large and spacious and the aquarist should refrain from handling

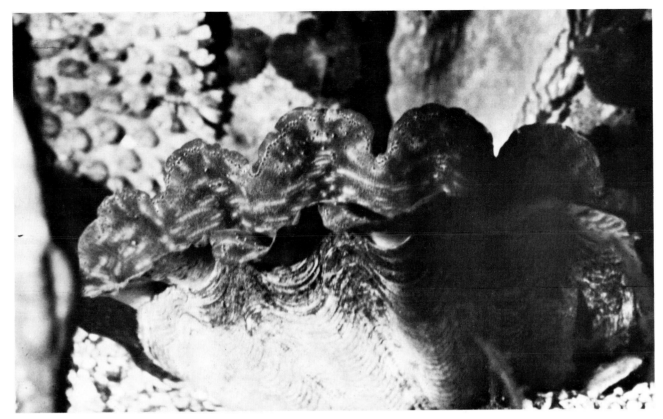

Frilly Clam, *Phylum mollusca*

them since many are poisonous, particularly the Blue Ringed Octopus (*Hapalochlaena maculosa*), whose bite is deadly.

Bivalve molluscs

This is a collective term used to encompass those animals which are clam-like or, in other words, have two shells surrounding their body. A typical example of this is the common mussel.

There are a great many species available in the shops, but probably the most popular and attractive is the Fire Clam or Rough Lima (*Lima scabra*). This mollusc, along with small clams such as the Bear Paw, may be kept in an aquarium. They are essentially filter-feeders and will thrive on a diet of liquid food intended for this sort of invertebrate.

Univalve molluscs

The univalve molluscs are those animals which have only one shell around their sac-like bodies.

A typical example of this type of animal is the common periwinkle. Their size may vary from a few millimeters, as in the bottom photograph overleaf, to the large Queen Conch which may be up to 1ft (300mm) long.

Many of them are highly coloured and some, like the cones, are extremely poisonous. They do make good additions to an invertebrate set-up where they will live on algae and the like.

Nudibranchs

This term has been used to describe those molluscs which have an internal shell or no shell at all. These animals include some of the most brightly coloured creatures on the earth. It seems a pity they are seldom seen by the average person. The nudibranch molluscs are ideally suited to life in an invertebrate aquarium and, because they are slow moving, can be observed quite closely. What strange creatures they are !

Most shrimps are highly coloured like this variety and in some cases may be bred in the aquarium

The Hermit Crabs can provide the aquarist with many happy hours of interest when their antics are observed
Photograph by Colin Nash

This tiny mollusc came into the aquarium on a piece of living rock and is only 4mm long

Coral Fishes Illustrated in Part 2

When referring to the popular names in this work it must be remembered that, in this case, there is no standardisation. Thus a popular name in the United States may differ from that of the same species in Australia or the United Kingdom. Moreover, it would be an impossible task to create a complete listing. It is for this reason that the reader is advised to familiarise himself with the latin names since these are accepted internationally.

Family	Latin name	Popular name
Acanthuridae (Surgeons and Tangs)	Acanthurus achilles	Achilles Tang or Red-tailed Surgeon
	Acanthurus bleekeri	Striped Surgeon
	Acanthurus coeruleus	Blue Tang
	Acanthurus glaucopareius	Powder-brown Tang or Golden-rimmed Surgeon
	Acanthurus leucosternum	Powder Blue Surgeon
	Acanthurus lineatus	Green-line Surgeon or Clown Surgeon
	Acanthurus gahhm	Black Surgeon Fish or Grey Surgeon
	Naso brevirostris	Unicorn Tang or Short-nosed Unicorn Tang
	Naso lituratus	Japanese Tang or Smoothhead Unicorn Fish
	Paracanthus theutis	Regal Tang, Morpho Butterfly or Blue Surgeon
	Zebrasoma flavescens	Yellow Tang
	Zebrasoma scopas	Mink Tang or Brown Tang
	Zebrasoma veliferum	Sailfin Tang
Apongonidae (Cardinalfish)	Sphaeramia nematopterus	Common Pyjama Cardinal Fish or Orbiculate Cardinal Fish
	Sphaeramia orbicularis	Mottled Cardinal
Balistidae (Triggerfish)	Amanses pardalis	Mottled Triggerfish or Variegated Trigger
	Balistapus undulatus	Undulated Triggerfish or Orange-green Triggerfish
	Balistes bursa	White-lined Triggerfish or Humuhumu Lei (Hawaiian)
	Balistes vetula	Queen Triggerfish, Old Wife, Old Wench, Cochino or Peje Puerco
	Balistoides conspiculum	Clown Triggerfish
	Melichthys vidua	Pink-tail Triggerfish

Balistidae (continued)	Odonus niger	Royal Blue Triggerfish, Redfang Triggerfish or Black Triggerfish
	Rhinecanthus aculeatus	Hawaiian Triggerfish or Humu-humu-nuku-nuku-a-puaa (Hawaiian)
	Rhinecanthus rectangulus	Belted Triggerfish
Blenniidae (Blennies)	Blennius pavo	Peacock Blenny
	Pholidichthys leucotaenia	Convict Blenny
Callyodontidae (Parrotfishes)	Bolbometopon bicolor	Two-coloured Parrotfish
	Scarus taeniopterus	Striped Parrotfish or Princess Parrotfish
Canthigasteridae, Diodontidae and Tetraodontidae	Arothron nigropunctatus	Yellow- or Black-spotted Puffer
	Canthigaster bennetti	Sharp Nose Puffer or Bennett's Sharp Nose Puffer
(Pufferfishes, Porcupinefishes and Blowfishes)	Canthigaster solandri	Sharp-nosed Puffer
	Canthigaster valentini	Sharp-nosed Puffer
	Diodon hystrix	Balloonfish or Porcupinefish
	Sphaeroides spengleri	Bandtail Puffer
	Tetraodon fluviatilis	Freshwater Pufferfish
Chaetodontidae (Butterflyfishes and Angelfishes)	Centropyge argi	Pygmy Angelfish or Cherubfish
	Centropyge bicolor	Bicolor Cherub, Oriole Angels, Two-coloured Angelfish or Vaqueta de Dos Colores
	Centropyge bispinosus	Coral Beauty or Dusky Angelfish
	Centropyge eibeli	Tiger Angelfish
	Centropyge ferrugatus	Rusty Angelfish
	Centropyge flavissimus	Lemonpeel Angel or Lemonpeel
	Centropyge vrolikii	Pearl-scaled Angelfish
	Chaetodon aurega	Threadfin, Diagonal Butterflyfish or Threadfin Butterflyfish
	Chaetodon capistratus	Mock Eye or Four-eyed Butterflyfish
	Chaetodon chrysurus	Orange Butterflyfish or Pearl-scale Butterfly
	Chaetodon citrinellus	Speckled Butterflyfish
	Chaetodon collaris	Pakistani Butterflyfish or Brown Butterflyfish
	Chaetodon ephippium	Saddle-back Butterflyfish or Black-blotched Butterflyfish
	Chaetodon falcula	Black-wedge Butterflyfish or Saddled Butterflyfish
	Chaetodon fasciatus	Diagonal-lined Butterflyfish
	Chaetodon fremblii	Blue-striped Butterflyfish
	Chaetodon klieni	Sunburst Butterflyfish
	Chaetodon larvatus	Blue Chevron Butterflyfish or Red Sea Butterflyfish

Chaetodontidae (continued)	Chaetodon lineolatus	Lined Butterflyfish
	Chaetodon lunula	Moon Butterflyfish or Red-striped Butterflyfish
	Chaetodon melanotus	Black-backed Butterflyfish
	Chaetodon miliaris	Lemon Butterflyfish
	Chaetodon pictus	as Latin name
	Chaetodon plebius	Coral Butterflyfish
	Chaetodon striatus	Puerto-Rican or Banded Butter-flyfish
	Chaetodon trifascialis	Chevron Butterflyfish
	Chaetodon trifasciatus	Rainbow Butterflyfish or Redfin Butterflyfish
	Chaetodon vagabundis	Vagabond Butterflyfish
	Chelmon rostratus	Chelmon, Copper-band Butterfly-fish
	Euxiphipops nevarchus	Majestic Angelfish or Blue-girdled Angelfish
	Euxiphipops sexstriatus	Six-barred Angelfish
	Euxiphipops xanthometapon	Blue-faced Angelfish or Yellow-faced Angelfish
	Forcipiger flavissimus	Long-nosed Butterflyfish
	Heniochus acuminatus	Bannerfish, Wimple or Poor Man's Moorish Idol
	Heniochus varius	Brown Wimple Fish or Humphead Banner Fish
	Holacanthus isabelita	Blue Angelfish
	Holacanthus ciliaris	Queen Angelfish
	Holacanthus townsendi	Townsend's Angelfish
	Holacanthus tricolor	Rock Beauty
	Holacanthus trimaculatus	Flagfin Angelfish or Three-spot Angelfish
	Parachaetodon ocellatus	Ocellate Butterflyfish
	Pomacanthus annularis	Blue-ring Angelfish
	Pomacanthus arcuatus	Black Angelfish or Gray Angelfish
	Pomacanthus imperator	Imperial Angelfish or Emperor Angelfish
	Pomacanthus maculosus	Purple Moon Angelfish or Blue Moon Angelfish
	Pomacanthus paru	French Angelfish
	Pomacanthus semicirculatus	Koran Angelfish or Semicircle Angelfish
	Prognathodes aculeatus	Atlantic Butterflyfish or Long-snout Butterflyfish
	Pygoplites diacanthus	Regal Angelfish or Royal Empress Angelfish
Gobiidae (Gobies)	Elactinus oceanops	Neon Goby
	Eleotrides strigatus	Golden-headed Sleeper
	Gobiodon citrinus	Yellow Goby or Goby
	Ptereleotris tricolor	Rocket, Arrowfish or Scissortail

Haemulidae and Plectorhynchidae (Grunts and Sweet lips)	Gaterin liniatus	Lined Sweetlips or Striped Sweetlips
	Haemulon flavoliniatum	French Grunt
	Plectorhynchus albovittatus	Yellow-lined Sweetlips
	Plectorhynchus chaetodonoides	Clown Sweetlips or Polka-dot Grunt
	Plectorhynchus orientalis	Oriental Sweetlips
	Spilotichthys pictus	Painted Sweetlips
Holocentridae (Squirrelfishes)	Adioryx diadema	Barred Squirrelfish
	Adioryx rubra	African Squirrelfish
	Adioryx spinifer	Long-jawed Squirrelfish
	Adioryx tiere	Palau Squirrelfish
	Holocentrus rufus	Squirrelfish
	Myripristes jacobus	Blackbar Soldierfish
Labridae (Wrasses)	Bodianus axillaris	Coral Hogfish
	Bodianus pulchellus	Spotfin or Cuban Hogfish
	Bodianus rufus	Spanish Hogfish
	Coris angulata	Twinspot Wrasse or Clown Labrid
	Coris formosa	African Clown Wrasse
	Coris gaimard	Red Labrid, Yellow-tailed Wrasse or Clown Wrasse
	Doratonotus megalepis	Green Wrasse or Dwarf Wrasse
	Hemipteronotus taeniurus	Dragon Wrasse
	Labroides bicolor	Bicolor Wrasse or Bicolored Cleaner Wrasse
	Labroides dimidiatus	Cleaner Wrasse or Bicolored Cleaner Wrasse
	Pseudocheilinus hexataenia	Pyjama Wrasse or Six-lined Wrasse
	Thallasoma bifasciatum	Blue Head
	Thallosoma lunare	Moon Wrasse, Lunar Wrasse or Lyretail Wrasse
	Thallasoma lutescens	Blue Fin or Banana Wrasse
Lutjanidae and Serranidae (Snappers, Groupers and Sea Basses)	Anthias squamipinnis	Wreckfish, Lyretail Coralfish or Butterfly Perch
	Chromileptis altivelis	Pantherfish or Polka-dot Grouper
	Gramma loreto	Royal Gramma or Fairy Basslet
	Lutjanus sebae	Emperor Snapper, Government Bream or Red Emperor
	Mirolabrichthys tuka	Purple Queen or Butterfly Perch as Latin name
	Pseudochromis dilectus	
	Pseudochromise paccagnellae	False Gramma, Dottyback, Royal Dottyback or Paccagnella's Dottyback
Monocanthidae (Filefishes)	Monacanthus spinosissimus	Tasseled Filefish
	Oxymoncanthus longirostris	Orange-green Filefish or Long-nosed Filefish

Monocanthidae (continued)	Pervagor tomentosus	Pink-tailed Filefish or Red-tailed Filefish
Monodactylidae and Scatophagidae (Monos and Scats)	Microcanthus strigatus Monodactylus argenteus Monodactylus sebae Scatophagus argus	Stripey Mono or Malayan Angelfish Sea Bat or Moonfish Scat or Spotted Scat
Muraenidae (Moray Eels)	Echidna zebra Rhinomuraena amboinensis	Zebra Moray Blue Ribbon Eel
Ostraciidae (Trunkfishes)	Lactoria fornasini Ostracion cubis	Cowfish or Short-horned Cowfish Spotted Cube
Platacidae (Batfishes)	Platax orbicularis Platax pinnatus Platax teira	Batfish or Orbiculate Batfish Batfish or Long-finned Batfish Batfish or Long-finned Batfish
Plotosidae (Catfish)	Plotosus anguillaris	Coral Catfish, Candy-striped Catfish or Salt-water Catfish
Pomacentridae (Demoiselles and Clownfishes)	Glyphidodontops cyaneus Abudefduf biocellatus Abudefduf hemicyaneus Abudefduf leucogaster Abudefduf oxyodon Abudefduf saxatilis Abudefduf sordidus Amphiprion akindynos Amphiprion (Premnas) biaculeatus Amphiprion clarkii Amphiprion ephippium Amphiprion frenatus Amphiprion latezonatus Amphiprion melanopus Amphiprion ocellaris Amphiprion poridoraion Amphiprion polymnus Amphiprion sandaracinos Amphiprion Sebae Amphiprion tricinctus Chromis caeruleus	Blue Devil as Latin name Yellow-tailed Blue Damsel Yellow Belly Devil Neon Damsel or Blue Velvet Damsel Sergeant Major Kupipi Barrier Reef Anemonefish Premnas, Maroon Clownfish or Spine-cheeked Anemonefish Black Clown, Brown Anemone-fish or Chocolate Clownfish Saddle Anemonefish Fire Clown, Tomato Clown or Red Clown Wide-band Anemonefish Fire Clown Clown Anemonefish or Common Clown Pink Skunk Clown, White-banded Anemonefish or False Skunk-striped Anemonefish Saddle-back Clown Yellow Skunk Clown Sebae Clown or Brown Clown Maroon Clown Green Chromis or Blue-green Chromis

Pomacentridae	Chromis cyanea	Blue Chromis or Blue-forked Tail Damsel
(continued)	Dascyllus aruanus	Humbug Damsel, Black and White Damsel or White-tailed Damselfish
	Dascyllus carneus	Cloudy Damselfish, Freckled Damselfish, White-tailed Dascyllus or Blue-top Damselfish
	Dascyllus melanurus	Four-striped Damsel, Black-tailed Dascyllus or Black-tailed Humbug
	Dascyllus trimaculatus	Three-spot Damsel or Domino Damsel
	Glyhidodontops hemicyaneus	Bicolor Damsel
	Neopomacentrus azysron	as Latin name
	Paraglyphidodon behni	Black and Gold Damsel
	Paraglyphidodon melanopus	Bowtie Damsel or Bluefin Damsel
	Pomacentrus amboinensis	Yellow Damsel
	Pomacentrus coeruleus	Electric Blue Damselfish or Blue Devil
	Pomacentrus melanochir	Yellow-tailed Blue Damsel or Saffron Blue Damsel
Sciaenidae (Drums or Croakers)	Equetus acuminatus	Cubbyu or High-hat
Scorpaenidae (Scorpionfish)	Dendrochirus zebra	Dwarf Lionfish or Zebra Lionfish
	Pterois antennata	Spotfin Lionfish
	Pterois lunulata	Scorpionfish
	Pterois volitans	Peacock Lionfish, Scorpionfish, Turkeyfish or Butterfly Cod
Syngnathidae (Sea Horses and Pipefishes)	Dunkerocampus dactyliophorus	Zebra Pipefish
	Hippocampus brevirostris	Short-snouted Sea Horse
	Hippocampus hudsonius	Atlantic Sea Horse or Northern Sea Horse
	Hippocampus kuda	Yellow Sea Horse or Oceanic Sea Horse
Zanclidae (Moorish Idols)	Zanclus canescens	Zanclus, Moorish Idol or Toby

Glossary

Acclimatisation: The process of gradual introduction of a newly acquired fish or invertebrate to its aquarium. Normally done by allowing the water in the aquarium to mix slowly with the water containing the animal thus ensuring that any change in water takes place over hours rather than seconds.

Acid water: Water from an area rich in peat is acidic, and will give a reading between 0 and 7 on a pH scale.

Activated charcoal: A filter medium normally used in external filters. Particularly suited to the removal of phenol-based impurities in sea water (seen as a yellowish discolouration of the water).

Adipose fin: A small fleshy fin on the back of some fishes, situated behind the dorsal fin.

Adjuster: See *Buffer.*

Aeration: A process of maintaining the oxygen level of the water by pushing air bubbles up through it. This method of aeration only assists the natural process of oxygen absorption.

Aerobic bacteria: Bacteria which thrive on oxygen and break down organic wastes into inert solids.

Air bladder: Sometimes called the swim bladder, it is a bladder filled with gas in the body cavity of most fishes, serving to compensate for the weight of the fish itself.

Air lift: The prime mover of most air-operated water filters, in that water is lifted up a tube by air bubbles striving to reach the surface.

Airstone: A porous block of wood or stone fixed to the end of an air tube. In an aquarium this is used to dissipate air bubbles into a fine cloud of much smaller bubbles.

Algae: Plant life having no roots, including a wide variety of seaweeds.

Alkali water: Water from a limestone, chalky or calcareous area, reading between 8 and 14 on the pH scale.

Alkalinity reserve: A measure of the buffering capacity. The amount of alkaline substance which may be added without effecting a change in the pH. See *Buffering capacity.*

Anaerobic bacteria: Bacteria which are poisoned by oxygen. They are harmful, and usually cause disease.

Anterior: Pertaining to the front.

Anus: See *Vent.*

Bacterial colonies: A number of bacteria which exist as a reproductive, and thus growing group.

Bacterial cultures: A colony of bacteria grown deliberately and often in controlled conditions.

Bar: A vertical colour mark with straight sides.

Barbel: A tentacle-like appendage on the chin of some fishes, its function being for sensory purposes.

Base medium: Material such as shell, gravel or sand used to cover the floor of an aquarium.

Bio-system: The term used to describe an aquarium employing natural or semi-natural filtration.

Bivalve: An animal having a shell in two valves or parts, like the oyster.

Brackish: A mixture of sea water and fresh water found in estuaries and the like.

Brine shrimp: A small marine crustacean (*Artemia salina*) used as food for fish. Normally the eggs are purchased and hatched out by the aquarist in a salt solution after which they can be netted out of the hatching container and used as starter-food for finicky feeding fish.

Brine shrimp nauplii: The larvae of the brine shrimp.

Brood pouch: A pouch in which the eggs are laid, and which hatch there. Often the young will remain in the brood pouch after hatching in order to be protected by one of their parents (usually the male of the species).

Bottom feeder: A fish which feeds from the

bottom of the aquarium, taking up that which has dropped to the floor of the tank.

Buffer: A concentrated solution of salts used to raise the pH of sea water to the required level. Usually buffers are added on a regular basis to replace salts which are used up by plants and animals, thus making the water less alkaline. Also known as adjusters.

Buffering capacity: The amount of alkaline salts present in the water to counteract any trend towards acidity. See *Alkaline reserve.*

Calcareous: Containing chalk or lime.

Calcium content: The amount of this metal present in chalk and lime.

Calibrated chart: A chart in which the graduations allow for irregularities.

Carnivore: A flesh eater.

Caudal fin: Tail fin.

Caudal peduncle: That part of the body at the base of the tail, normally the narrowest doint.

Chloride cells: These cells are found in the gills of a fish and are used for excreting salt from the body.

Closed system: A system where some processes are artificially regulated, relying upon itself, as a system, for its own balance and survival.

Cnidoblast: With the nematocyst, forms part of the stinging cell of the sea anemone.

Coarse medium: Coarsely crushed shell, or gravel which may form a base medium at the bottom of the tank. The larger size of these particles prevents them from being sucked up the filter.

Commensalism: A form of symbiosis in which only one of the animals benefits from the relationship.

Community tank: An aquarium containing several different species of fishes living in peaceful coexistence.

Compressed: Laterally flattened.

Condensation: The warm moist air which evaporates from the water in the tank, meets the cooler metal top or sides of the tank and returns as vapour once more to water as it cools.

Copper sulphate: A blue, crystalline poison. It has fungicide properties but should not be used without expert advice.

Coral sand: Sand which is formed by coral that has been broken down into fine sandy particles.

Cure: Set, to a hard waterproof finish.

Cutting: Artificially separating sponges in order to reproduce them. See *Separation.*

Daphnia: A small freshwater flea of questionable value as food for coral fishes.

Dendritic organ: An organ composed of cells similar to the chloride cells in the gill filaments of fishes and the salt cells of birds. Found in *Plotosus anguillaris,* this organ is located just behind the vent. It is suggested that this organ functions as a salt secreting gland and is found in both sexes.

Depressed: Vertically flattened.

Dimorphic: A species in which there is a marked difference in the appearance of the two sexes.

Dip tube: A capilliary or pipe-shaped tube used to draw water out of an aquarium.

Diseaseolve: A commercially prepared medication.

Dorsal: Pertaining to the upper part of the body.

Dorsal fin: The fin on the back of a fish. There are often two, anterior and posterior, dorsal fins.

Ectoparasite: An external parasite, one which lives on the outside of the body.

Emaciated: Of a starved appearance. This usually means that the fish is not feeding and has not fed for some time.

Evaporation: In which water molecules are captured by the warmer air causing them to become water vapour. This leads to the actual amount of water constantly decreasing.

External skeletons: The outer carapace or shell of animals such as crabs or prawns.

Fairy shrimp: A small crustacean used as a food for fishes.

Family: A collective term used to incorporate all similar genera into one group of like-creatures.

Filter base: A porous plate through which the water is drawn.

Filter bed: The filtering medium which removes the debris from the water.

Filter box: The box containing the filter.

Filter feeding invertebrates: In such animals as sponges which live as a permanent and interdependent colony, the water is drawn in through tiny pores leaving the tiny food particles for the individual animals to feed upon. The filtered water is then ejected through larger pores, or sometimes a central channel within the colony.

Filter wool: See *Nylon wool.*

Filtration: The removal of unwanted matter from a solution.

Flake foods: Commercially prepared dried fish food in flake form.

Fluorescent illumination: Brighter lighting obtained, for the same consumption of electricity, by using fluorescent materials to convert ultraviolet radiation in the electric lamp into visible light.

Food chain: A biological cycle which, in simplified form, could be described as bacteria being eaten by small organisms, which are in their turn eaten by small fishes, which are eaten by big fishes, which die and whose decaying bodies are fed upon by bacteria.

Forked: Angled inwards.

Freeze-dried aquarium foods: Dried food for marine fishes. This type of food reconstitutes itself on contact with water.

Fresh protein: Normally used to describe live food such as shrimps or frozen food such as mussels, squid, razor meat, cockles, mysid shrimps and the like.

Fry: Young fish, normally free swimming.

Genera: A collective term used to incorporate like-species into one group. The first part of the Latin name of any creature refers to the genus and is capitalised, the second part refers to the species.

Genus: The singular of genera.

Gill: An opening containing membranes with the function of providing respiration.

Harvesting algae: Removing excess algae growth.

Herbivore: A plant eater.

Hydrometer: A calibrated instrument for measuring the specific gravity of a liquid, in this case salt water.

Ichthyology: The science and study of fishes.

Immersion heater: A heater which is placed in the water.

Incandescent illumination: Where the light is produced by heating a filament to white or red heat usually, in lighting, by the passage of an electric current.

Inert solids: Particles which are inactive chemically and therefore safe.

Interorbital space: The space at the top of the head between the eyes.

Invertebrates: Animals without backbones.

Lamina: A thin layer or bone, scale or membrane.

Lateral: Pertaining to the side.

Lateral line: A sensory canal running along the sides of a fish.

Lethal saturation: Where a toxic substance builds up in the water to a level where it is deadly.

Life-support system: A system where the conditions required to support life are produced artificially.

Liquid food: A commercially prepared liquid nutrient, of most use with fry and invertebrates. Sometimes called liquid fry food.

Liquid fry food: See *Liquid food.*

Live food: Animals which are fed to the fishes whilst alive, such as mysus shrimp, brine shrimp, tubifex or daphnia.

Metabolic process: The chemical changes and processes which take place in the cells or bodies of living creatures.

Micro animals: Animals which are so small that they are usually only visible under a microscope.

Mouth brooder: A fish which cares for its eggs by carrying them in its mouth until they hatch.

Mucous cocoon: A protective barrier or layer which the fish produces by excreting mucus from pores in its skin. This may also hide the scent of the fish.

Mutualism: A form of symbiosis where both species involved benefit from the partnership.

Mysus shrimp: A popular name amongst aquarists, it is used to describe mysid shrimp, a small crustacean used as food for fish.

Nape: The dorsal part of the head.

Nematocyst: See *Cnidoblast.*

Nitrates: Salts which have fertilising properties and are beneficial to plant life in an aquarium, and therefore to the bio-system, if kept at a controlled level. It is important to remember that many fishes will not tolerate a high level of nitrates.

Nitrite: A cumulative compound which, if the level is allowed to build up, will weaken the fishes and eventually cause their death.

Nitrogenous toxins: Poisons caused by a build-up of the nitrogen level in a tank.

Nylon wool: Commercially packed nylon fibre which is used as part of a filter system.

Ocellus: An eye-like colour marking.

Omnilogical filtration: Filtration using both plant and animal biological processes.

Omnivore: A plant and flesh eater.

Oolite: Coral sand.

Operculum: Gill cover.

Oral disc: The 'mouth' of a sea anemone, an elastic membrane which surrounds the circular opening of the body cavity.

Oxidisation: The process by which oxygen combines with metal to form rust.

Ozone: An unstable form of oxygen (O_3) in the atmosphere. A poisonous gas which, in controlled doses, may be useful for killing bacteria.

Ozone reactor: An aquarium appliance used to diffuse ozone into the water.

Parasite: An organism which lives off other organisms.

Pathogenic bacteria: Disease-causing bacteria.

Pectoral fin: Situated on each side of the body behind the operculum.

Pedal disc: The foot or base of the sea anemone.

Pelagic: Free floating at the mercy of the tide or currents.

Pelvic fin: Situated as a pair in front of the vent, also called ventral fins.

Permeable: Porous, through which molecules may pass.

pH: A unitless index from 0 to 14 used to describe the degree of acidity or alkalinity of a substance. 0 is the highest degree of acidity and 14 is the highest degree of alkalinity, a pH of 7 being the neutral point,

related by formula to a standard solution of potassium hydrogen phtholate which has a value of 4 at 15° Centigrade.

Phyla: The basic sub-division of the animal kingdom. There are twenty-five of these groups.

Phylum: The singular of phyla.

Pipette: A small glass tube with a narrowed end and a rubber air bag on the other end. It is used by expelling the air from the bag out through the tube and then releasing the bag, causing water, and any object in the water small enough, to be sucked up the tube.

Piston pump: An air pump driven by one or two pistons.

Plankton: Micro animals which live in sea water and which provide a rich source of nourishment for many species of marine life.

Polyp: A many-tentacled animal usually living in colonies, some of which form the calcareous structure of coral.

Power filters: The power of the filter refers to the rate (in gallons or litres per hour) at which water is passed through the filter medium.

Predacean: An animal which is predatory.

Predator: An animal which hunts to catch food.

Proteinous deposit: A deposit of proteinous matter.

Proteinous matter: After water has been removed, protein is the substance which forms the major part of any living organism. Protein is high in nitrogen, so dead and decaying material will also be high in nitrogen ; therefore proteinous matter is potentially dangerous.

Protein skimmer: A device designed to reduce the amount of proteinous matter in the aquarium.

Protozoa: Unicellular or one-celled organisms.

Quarantine: The isolation of fishes to prevent the spread of disease in an already established aquarium.

Radial symmetry: Symmetry of a circular nature radiating from a central point, as seen in starfishes, sea urchins and jellyfish.

Ray: The bony support of the fin.

Reagent: A substance which has a known

reaction to a given chemical or condition in the water.

Schooling: An instinct in some species of fish to swim in groups (these groups may be quite small or very large). Also called shoaling.

Sea-salt mixes: Commercially prepared mixtures designed to reproduce a correct sea-water balance when mixed with fresh water.

Separation: Sponges reproduce their colonies by a section of sponge growing away from the main body and eventually, when it has established its own base on a rock or the surface, separating from it.

Shoaling: See *Schooling.*

Silica sand: Formed by the erosion of sandstone and other amorphous forms of silica.

Silicone sealers: A commercially produced waterproof plastic which is derived from silicon, a non-metallic element.

Siphon: A tube of plastic. One end is placed in a container at a level lower than the water level of the aquarium and the other end is placed in the aquarium. Gravity causes the water to run from the aquarium into the tube and to the container. Unwanted food and other substances may be sucked into the tube.

Snout: That part of the head in front of the eye.

Sodium cyanide: A drug which is used for rendering fishes unconscious in order to catch them. This is often harmful to the fishes, and many may succumb to this or other such drugs after they have been purchased by the aquarist.

Species: A group of individuals having common characteristics, specialised from others of the genus.

Specific gravity: The weight of a substance when compared to that of pure water at standard pressure and temperature ($4°C$) eg SG $1·022 = 1·022$ times heavier than pure water at $4°C$.

Spectrum analysis: An analysis or chart showing the spectrum (from infra-red to ultra-violet).

Stripe: A horizontal colour marking.

Sub-species: A division in a species where the differences are not enough to create two separate species.

Superorbital tentacles: Tentacles rising from the area above the eye socket.

Swim bladder: See *Air bladder.*

Symbiosis: Two different kinds of animal living and associating together.

Synonym: A scientific name that is invalid, normally proposed after the accepted name.

Toxic: Poisonous.

Trigger mechanism: A modified dorsal spine which can be erected and locked in position.

Tube feet: The small projections underneath such animals as starfish which provide them with locomotion.

Tubercles: Small swellings.

Tubifex: A small reddish-brown worm, mud dwelling in origin and used by aquarists as food for fish.

Turnover rate: The number of gallons (or litres) which pass through a filter in an hour.

Ultra-violet lamp: A lamp which gives off ultra-violet rays which are the radiations of wavelengths less then those of visible light.

Ultra-violet steriliser: A piece of equipment which allows water to be pumped round an ultra-violet lamp which has the effect of killing protozoa and bacteria which pass it.

Undergravel filters: Filters which are placed between the glass of the tank floor and the base medium of the gravel.

Unstable gas: A gas whose molecules may split up into their component atoms (which may recombine to form different molecules) generally owing to a change in an external circumstance, usually temperature.

Vent: The opening at the end of the digestive tract from which waste matter is expelled.

Ventral: Opposite to dorsal, the lower part of the body.

Vibrator action: Pumping action caused by the vibrating of a diaphragm, powered by electricity.

Yolk-sac: The yolk containing sac which is attached to the embryo, in this case newly born fry.

Conversion Tables

Inches	Millimetres
$\frac{1}{2}$	12·70
1	25·40
$1\frac{1}{2}$	38·10
2	50·80
$2\frac{1}{2}$	63·50
3	76·20
$3\frac{1}{2}$	88·90
4	101·60
$4\frac{1}{2}$	114·30
5	127·00
$5\frac{1}{2}$	139·70
6	152·40
$6\frac{1}{2}$	165·10
7	177·80
$7\frac{1}{2}$	190·50
8	203·20
$8\frac{1}{2}$	215·90
9	228·60
$9\frac{1}{2}$	241·30
10	254·00
11	279·40
12	304·80
13	330·20
14	355·60
15	381·00
16	406·40
17	431·80
18	457·20
19	482·60
20	508·00
21	533·40
22	558·80
23	584·20
24	609·60
25	635·00
26	660·40
27	685·80
28	711·20
29	736·60
30	762·00

Gallons	Litres
20	90·92
25	113·65
30	136·38
35	159·11
40	181·84
45	204·57
50	227·30
55	250·03
60	272·76

Further Reading

Anemonefishes, G. R. Allen. TFH Publications (1972)

Aquarist's Encyclopaedia, Sterba. Blandford (1983)

Aquarium Fishes, Dick Mills. Kingfisher Books (1980)

Aquarium Fishes, Gwynne Vevers. Mitchell Beazley (1980)

Butterflyfishes and Angelfishes of the World, volumes 1 & 2, Roger C. Steene & G. R. Allen. Hans A. Baensch (1977)

Caribbean Reef Fishes, John E. Randall. TFH Publications (1968)

Damselfishes of the South Seas, G. R. Allen. TFH Publications (1975)

Ecology of Fishes in Tropical Waters. Edward Arnold (1977)

The Ocean World of Jacques Cousteau (various volumes), Jacques-Yves Cousteau. Angus and Robertson (1975)

Sea Anemones, U. Erich Friese. TFH Publications (1972)

Seashells, R. Tucker Abbott. Bantam Books (1976)

Seawater Aquariums, Spotte. Wiley (1979)

Tropical Fish in your Home, Axelrod & Burgess. Sterling (USA) (1980)

World Encyclopaedia of Fishes, Alwynne Wheeler. Macdonald (1985)

The British Marine Aquarists Association

If you have enjoyed this book and would like further information you may like to join the above society.

It is an association which caters for the needs of tropical and native marine aquarists in the UK. Membership is open to both beginners and advanced specialists and includes members from Australia, USA, Canada and Hong Kong. The necessary forms can be obtained by writing to: John H. Vickery, National Secretary, BMAA, 26 Rosalind Avenue, Dudley, West Midlands, DY1 4JW, England

Acknowledgements

My sincere thanks are extended to Dr Gerald R. Allen, of the Department of Ichthyology, The Western Australian Museum, Perth ; Dr John E. Randall, of the Bernice P. Bishop Museum, Hawaii, USA ; Dr Martin R. Brittan, Department of Biological Sciences, California State University, Sacramento, USA, and to his friend Richard Ashby. I owe gratitude also to Mrs Gay Ellis, of Soest, West Germany ; Herr Bartmeier, of Sudrings, Paderborn, West Germany ; Keith Foskett and his wife Ann, of the Wokingham Aquarium, Berkshire ; to Mr S. Prescott and to Colin Nash ; and Mr B. Lonsdale, coral importer, of Heywood, Lancs. I am also indebted to Graham F. Cox and SeAquariums Waterlife Research ; also to my own brother, Tony Hargreaves. Special thanks, though, are extended to my immediate family, especially my wife Margaret, without whose patience, encouragement and criticism this book would never have been completed.

Index